Thoughts Along the Way

Devotionals for Spiritual Nourishment

By Elaine Mehn

Published by Gospel Rest Resources

Thoughts Along the Way: Devotions for Spiritual Nourishment

ISBN 0-9722861-0-1

Copyright © 2002 by Elaine Mehn, All Rights Reserved. No part of this book may be reproduced in any form or by any electronic or mechanical means, including information storage and retrieval systems, without written permission from the publisher, except as provided by USA copyright law.

Scripture quotations in this book unless otherwise noted are taken from the HOLY BIBLE, NEW INTERNATIONAL VERSION. Copyright © 1973, 1978, 1984 by International Bible Society. Used by permission of Zondervan Bible Publishers.

First printing 2002

Library of Congress Control Number: 2002093088

Cover art by Elizabeth Louise Mehn
Cover Design by Jim Rew

Printed in the U.S.A. by Morris Publishing
3212 E. Hwy 30, Kearney, NE 68847
(800) 650-7888

Dedication

To my loving husband
who struggles with me
to daily live in God's grace
and to my children, Tim and Beth,
who are God's love blessing to me.

I want to especially thank my family for loving me in my struggles and letting me use their stories in my writing. God truly blessed me when He put me in such a wonderful family. I also want to thank all of those who helped to make this book a reality. Susan and Bruce Young who reintroduced me to the wonders of God's grace, Steve Childers for his encouragement to put these devotions together in a book, Jim Rew for his expertise and layout, Bruce Young for his editing, Gary Fujino and Connie Matsumoto for proof reading, and all of those who read e-mail "Thoughts Along the Way" and encouraged me to continue writing.

Contents

Introduction   7

Thoughts Along the Way   8

Holiday Thoughts Along the Way   104

Index of Themes   113

Index of Scriptures   115

Order Form   119

Introduction

Thoughts Along the Way started as personal journal reflections on the events of my life and how the Gospel was shaping my responses to those events. As I wrote more and more of these I started sending out weekly devotions by e-mail. I have continued this pattern by including a total of 52 devotions. The ones for specific holidays are in a separate section in the back of the book. I have also included an Index of Themes and an Index of Scriptures. I hope these will be helpful.

My prayer for you as you read this book is that God will give you a heart for the Gospel; a heart that doesn't just know the right things but its very existence depends on Christ. I pray that you will be consumed with love for Jesus and because of His great love you will be able to love others as well. May God give you a heart that is on fire with the grace of His Gospel, eyes to see your sins through God's eyes, the joy of repentance, and faith to know Him as you go along the way.

At the time of this printing I continue to send out weekly *Thoughts Along the Way*. If you would like to receive these by e-mail, please send your e-mail address to Gospel Rest Resources at GospelRestResources@Yahoo.com.

THOUGHTS ALONG THE WAY

Teach them to your children, talking about them when you sit at home and when you walk along the road, when you lie down and when you get up. Deuteronomy 11:19

On one of our home assignments from Japan we spent the summer months in Colorado. An older lady from the church we were visiting offered to take a couple of us hiking in the mountains. In Tokyo we live close to sea level so hiking in the Colorado mountains may not have been the smartest thing to do. I enjoy walking and readily agreed to go. It was a beautiful day for a hike. The trail she had chosen was not difficult but it did go up and up in elevation. It wandered through the trees, with clumps of flowers beside the trail. She explained to us novices her theory of hiking. She said you hike until you start to get tired then you stop and enjoy the flowers and plants. We stopped a lot because the Colorado mountains do not have enough air for us sea level types. She had been hiking for years and knew the names of all of the plants. As we hiked and rested she shared her knowledge with us and we all shared our lives with each other. God met us as we went along the way.

I often think of God meeting with me in church or in my personal devotions or at special retreats or conferences. He often does meet me at these times and teaches my heart great truths. He also desires to meet me as I go along the way each day. It is during the process of living each day and doing all of the things that need to be done that I need to meet with God. It is when I get tired of "doing" and realize my need for God that He meets me and shows me the "flowers" that He has put all around me. It is in these Thoughts Along the Way that I most often learn more of my Creator and my heart is touched by Him.

We can't always escape to the mountains but we can meet with God along the way no matter if that way is on city streets or country roads or even running down halls chasing an energetic 2 year old. God can meet us in hospital waiting rooms, in airports, or at home. All we have to do is take a deep breath and see what God wants to show us.

Prayer: Father, keep me from being so busy doing that I loose sight of You. Teach my heart and my eyes to see those things that You have put all around me. Teach me each day as I go along the way with You.

A New Day

The LORD bless you and keep you; the LORD make his face shine upon you and be gracious to you; the LORD turn his face toward you and give you peace. Numbers 6:24-26

This morning I decided to bake bread as a Saturday surprise for my family. The yeast was proofed and ready to use when I discovered that I didn't have enough flour. In Japan all of the stores open at 10:00 with the exception of a small grocery store near our house. I quickly grabbed my coat and dashed out to buy the needed flour. As I walked home from the store I was struck by the new day that was all around me. The sun was shining without a cloud in the sky. The various shopkeepers were preparing their stores to greet the day's customers. I could even smell the bread baking at the bakery. But most amazing were the friendly smiles and cheery voices that greeted me. The stores were not open yet and wouldn't be for nearly an hour but every one was welcoming. What a great way to start a new day!

I may not need to dash to the grocery store every morning. (I certainly hope I don't.) But I can have this morning greeting time each day. Rain or shine, God is waiting to share Himself with me. He has prepared a glorious day just for me and wants to start that day with His smile and greeting. He is never too busy to spend time with me. If the creator and maintainer of the universe is not too busy for me, how can I think that I am too busy for Him?

I am not saying that if you spend time with God each morning you will have wonderfully smooth, comfortable days. Just as some days bring sunshine while other days may bring rain, snow, sleet, hail or even tornadoes or earthquakes, some of our days may be smooth and some days may be hard in the extreme. Spending time with God will not change the day that He has prepared for you, but it will change the way you respond to that day. No matter what comes you can face it with God's smile in your heart. You know that you are not alone, but that the Father has sent His own Holy Spirit to live in you and go through each day with you. He can use the best of circumstances and the worst of circumstances to create Christ in you. All He asks is that you let Him.

Prayer: Father, thank You for the day that You have prepared for me. I don't yet know what it holds but I know that whatever it is You will be with me. I rejoice in knowing that You have chosen to spend the entire day by my side so that I will never be alone. Help me to choose to spend the day with You. As my day becomes busy, keep my heart rejoicing in the knowledge of how you have demonstrated Your love for me in Christ so that no matter what comes Your smile is shining in my heart.

CREATION OR THE CREATOR

They exchanged the truth of God for a lie, and worshipped and served created things rather than the Creator – who is forever praised. Amen.
Romans 1:25

I recently took a trip to Kyoto, Japan. It seems that there is a temple or shrine on almost every corner. Some had absolutely beautiful gardens that you could spend hours enjoying. As I walked through the fresh green gardens and listened to the birds and the cicadas singing, I was struck by man's seemingly inexhaustible ability to take God's creation and turn it into an idol. Traditional Shintoism believes that there are spirits in the trees and the rocks and all of nature. The Japanese worship these spirits. God did not create nature for us to worship it but rather for us to worship Him, the Creator. (Psalm 19:1-4)

I enjoy doing cross stitch and needlepoint pictures. In a way they are my creation. I spend many hours working on them and they often reflect a small part of my personality. I enjoy when people tell me they like a particular picture especially if it is a picture that I designed myself. But I would be surprised and upset if someone started telling one of my pictures how much they liked it for making itself the way it did. I would try to kindly remind the person that the needlepoint did not stitch itself, but rather I was the one that spent many hours putting each of the small stitches in place. If the person continued to praise the picture for creating itself, I would begin to wonder about their mental condition. The created always reflects the creator. It is not the creator but contains a small hint of who he/she may be. This is as true with cross-stitch pictures as with nature.

When we praise nature and ignore the Creator we are giving credit to the wrong thing. How very sad this must be for God – to have His creation praised but to be ignored as its creator. God has shown and told mankind that He is the Creator of all things yet man continues to praise the creation and pretend that God either does not exist or that the creation itself is god. God has not given up on us nor has he put us in mental institutions. He continues to love us even to the point of sending His own Son to live and die for us.

As a Christian it is easy to see how wrong other religions are in worshipping the creation. The real problem comes when I let God show me the things in my own life that I worship. I don't worship trees and rocks or statues made by man. I do catch myself or rather God catches me desiring the praise of man more than the praise of God. I struggle with the approval of man becoming the driving force in my life. Others are driven by pleasure, power, reputation, or possessions. These are idol worship. I am giving the creation that place that only God deserves to have. God created everything for His glory, to reveal a bit of who He is.

Now we see but a poor reflection as in a mirror; then we shall see face to face. Now I know in part; then I shall know fully, even as I am fully known. I Corinthians 13:12

Prayer: Father, forgive me for all of the times that I have turned to Your creation for satisfaction rather than looking to You the Creator. Create in my heart a burning desire to know You and worship You alone. When my heart affections wander from You, let me be quick to remember Your incredible grace and have it recapture my heart. Don't let me ever be content to simply know about You or to know the works of Your hands. Let my praise ever be to You.

A Darkened Room

This is the message we have heard from him and declare to you: God is light; in him there is no darkness at all. If we claim to have fellowship with him yet walk in the darkness, we lie and do not live by the truth. But if we walk in the light, as he is in the light, we have fellowship with one another, and the blood of Jesus, his Son, purifies us from all sin. I John 1: 5-7

Imagine entering a darkened room. This room has a dimmer switch so the lights can be gradually turned up or down. When you first enter the room it is completely dark. The lights are then turned on just enough that you can see that it has furniture and some major clutter. As the lights come up more you see the hanging wallpaper and the piles of garbage around the room. The light continues to increase and you see the dust on everything and then the spider webs. You think that you can now see all that is wrong with the room as it is more fully illuminated. Later you discover that there are rats. The floor seems soft in parts and you discover that it needs to be replaced. It not only needs to be replaced but the entire room has termites eating it. The rats have attacked the electric wires and they all have to be replaced. The first hard rain also shows that the roof leaks and the windows don't keep out the wind or the rain. In short there is nothing about the room that is in good condition. It needs to be torn down and built again.

This room that we have been looking at is my life. It is your life. Before we come to Christ the room is entirely dark. We have no idea that there is even a light switch to be turned on. When the Holy Spirit enters our lives, He shows us our sins. We are shocked and saddened to see that we are sinners before a holy God. It is at this point that we often put forth our resolutions to improve. We set our goals and the means for their accomplishment. We try harder than we have been to clean up this messy room. This is very discouraging work because we discover that even the simplest mess seems too much for us.

As we mature in our Christian walk, the Holy Spirit continues to turn His light on our hearts and we discover that we are more sinful than we ever suspected. The mess is much greater than we first thought. Perhaps this really is too much for us. We need to hire an interior decorator. We look to other Christians to help us deal with the sins in our lives. There often comes a point where we think that God surely has shown us all of the bad stuff. There can't possibly any more. It is at this point that we realize that we do not need an interior decorator but a master builder. We are sinful to our very core.

Praise God that He knew all along that we needed a builder and not just a fix-it-upper. He sent His Son to die for all of our sins - the ones we see and the ones we don't see. Just because we don't see that the wiring is bad doesn't make the wiring OK. But Jesus did more than just provide a means of forgiveness of sin. God has also given us Jesus' righteousness. He has provided the Holy Spirit to be the master builder that we need. He can show us the things that need to be replaced and then work in us to replace them with Christ Himself.

Prayer: Father, I don't like to see my sins. I often don't want the Holy Spirit to turn the lights up because I don't want to see what is really there. Forgive my lack of love for You which makes me hate my sins and send the Holy Spirit to empower me to overcome the sins the light exposes. I know it can be painful but the result is worth the discomfort. Someday when I see You face to face I will see the entire room as You intend for it to be. Until then keep me in the rebuilding phase. May I never tire of living in the light.

WHEN SIGHT IS FAITH

When the Lord heard what you said, he was angry and solemnly swore: "Not a man of this evil generation shall see the good land I swore to give your forefathers." "And the little ones that you said would be taken captive, your children who do not yet know good from bad–they will enter the land. I will give it to them and they will take possession of it." Deuteronomy 1:34-35, 39

God had done miracle upon miracle in order to free the Israelites from Egypt. The Israelites had seen the plagues against the Egyptians, had received the riches of the Egyptians, when all looked hopeless had seen the Red Sea parted, had been led by a cloud by day and a pillar of fire by night, had been fed manna from heaven, and saw water flow from a rock. It is these same people who refused to believe that God could give them the Promised Land. Because of their unbelief God became angry with them and refused to let any of them inherit the land. He sent them into the desert for forty years until they all had died. He then gave the land to their children. Seeing all of these miracles was not enough to produce faith in the heart of these Israelites. They needed God to do the miracle of producing faith in their hearts.

    I used to wear contact lenses, the old hard kind. I was not the best user, as I was known to over wear them a great deal. On one particular occasion I had definitely over worn them and had small corneal abrasions. These are very painful and take some time to heal as I had found out on previous occurrences. A friend of mine had recently become a Christian and had been witnessing to me. She kept telling me that God was the same today as He was in the Bible. I knew from attending church as a child that Jesus healed people. I sat at my desk at work and prayed that if God were real he would show me by healing my eyes. To my utter amazement my eyes were healed the next morning. I, like the Israelites, had seen God produce a miracle and, as in the case of the Israelites, I was surprised, thankful, and confused but it did not produce faith. Faith came later as I drove to work. God did the real miracle of putting the pieces together for me and giving me a transformed heart.

Faith based only on miracles that can be seen is not real faith but sight. Often when the miracles stop the faith stops also. I am thankful that God did and still does miracles in my life and in the world. But I am eternally grateful that God did and still does give the miraculous gift of faith. Without this a miracle is simply something that cannot be explained.

Prayer: Father, I thank You that You gave me the faith to believe in You and I ask that You continue to grow that faith. Let me base my life on faith not sight even when that sight includes miracles.

SNIFF IT
DON'T DRINK IT

But whatever was to my profit I now consider loss for the sake of Christ. What is more, I consider everything a loss compared to the surpassing greatness of knowing Christ Jesus my Lord, for whose sake I have lost all things. I consider them rubbish that I may gain Christ and be found in him, not having a righteousness of my own that comes from the law, but that which is through faith in Christ–the righteousness that comes from God and is by faith. Philippians 3:7-9

"You do not serve Jesus out of giftedness but out of brokenness." I once heard a speaker say this. At the time I mentally said, "Yes that is right." and wrote the words in a notebook. That was the last I thought about it until recently when I was looking through that same notebook to see how much room was left or if I needed to buy a new one soon. What a blessed surprise it was to stumble across those words again.

    All through my life I have struggled with pride. At times it has come across as false humility and there have been times when I simply pretended that it was not a problem because I deserved praise. Looking back I feel sorry for the people who had to be around me as I was probably not the easiest person to befriend. Yes, I did have good grades in school, I am a good cook, I can sew and I enjoy designing and stitching cross-stitch, I have some ability to speak and am learning to write. Like the apostle Paul I am learning to count all these things as nothing compared to knowing Christ Jesus. All of my "natural" abilities and all of my "spiritual" giftedness are from God. I didn't produce them apart from God and I can't use them in His service apart from the Father.

    Howard Hendricks once said that praise is like fine perfume.

You need to sniff it not drink it. Whenever someone praises me, I remind myself that it is OK to enjoy the praise as one would enjoy smelling fine perfume but that I can't drink it. Drinking perfume is deadly just as drinking praise is deadly. Proverbs 18:12 "Before his downfall a man's heart is proud, but humility comes before honor." God gave me my abilities and created the situations in which I use them. The praise goes to Him not out of false pride and a need to show others how religious I am, but from a heart that knows that I am simply a loved sinner whom God has gifted. My joy, contentment, satisfaction, and fulfillment come from being graced. It's a "God thing" not an Elaine thing.

Prayer: Father, teach my heart true humility that I may praise you the giver of all good gifts. Keep me from expecting and needing the praise of others. Rather let me be content in doing what pleases you. Thank you for the gifts that you give and for the gifts that in your wisdom you do not give.

ENGAGEMENTS

Let us rejoice and be glad and give him glory! For the wedding of the Lamb has come, and his bride has made herself ready. Revelation 19:7

Those of you who are married, do you remember when you got engaged? Those of you who are not married will have to be creative in your memory. Remember the tender look of love mixed with fear. "What if she says, 'No!'" This is followed by the look of love mixed with fear. "She said, 'Yes!' What have I gotten myself into?" Often times this scene is accompanied by the giving of an engagement ring. (John was a poor seminary student so I got my engagement ring for Christmas after we had been married 5 years.)

Assuming she says yes, why does she? Is it so that she can keep this wonderful diamond ring? Is it because she loves and wants the giver of the ring? Why does he give the ring? Is it so he will have someone to cook for him and clean up after him? Is it because he loves her and can't image going through life without her by his side? If it is just for the ring or for the work, the marriage has a big problem before it even begins. Most people marry because they love each other and want to spend their lives together, not because they want an expensive ring or a live in house keeper.

Scripture often refers to believers as the bride of Christ. In laying down His life for us, He proposed to His wayward and headstrong bride. He did this not so that He would have diligent workers here on earth. It's a good thing because often His bride is less than diligent. He laid down His very life because He loves us and wants us to spend eternity with Him. When we accepted Christ's gift of forgiveness and eternal life, we accepted His proposal. Just as young couples getting engaged do not know all that is involved in marriage, we did not and still do not know all that is involved in being the bride of Christ. Some people may accept Christ so that they will attain heaven. This would be like agreeing to marry so that you can get the ring or the housekeeper. We may have accepted Christianity for very selfish reasons but we must grow beyond that to an unselfish response that comes out of a heart that has been touched by God's own love.

Marriage is not a simple, "I do." It is a day- by- day process of learning to love the other more than you love yourself. This does not happen on your wedding day but takes all of your years together and more. It is a process that sometimes goes fairly smoothly and sometimes is like death itself. Learning to be the bride of Christ is also a process. It does not happen in its entirety when we first believe. That is a beginning but it will take all of our life on earth to come to a deeper grasp and appreciation of God's grace and to respond with the love that He deserves. There are times when it seems easy to live a Christian life and there are times when it feels like death. If the death is to our own self and leads to life in Christ, we can rejoice even in the midst of pain.

Prayer: Father, You know my heart. I don't like pain or hard times. I also don't love You the way You deserve to be loved. Forgive my self-centeredness and work in my heart to create the bride who loves You for who You are rather than for the blessings that You give. Help me to take my focus off me and to see Your incredible grace, oh Creator and Lover of my soul!

"Glad to See Ya"

Offer hospitality to one another without grumbling. I Peter 4:9

Keep on loving each other as brothers. Do not forget to entertain strangers, for by so doing some people have entertained angels without knowing it. Hebrews 13:1-2

In "Startled by Silence" Ruth Senter tells of an elderly man who shuffles to the door and greets her with, "Come in. Come in. S'glad to see ya. Glad to see ya." This man not only welcomed her into his home; he was glad to see her and spend time with her. As I read this I thought over the last 24 hours and how I had greeted people who rang my doorbell. The first was my husband. When I saw that it was him, I'm embarrassed to say, I opened the door, turned and walked back into the living room grumbling about how he could be so lazy that he couldn't unlock the door. Hardly a word of welcome passed my lips. It turned out that he had forgotten to take his key. He was looking forward to getting home after a long day. Instead of coming "home", he came to a "house".

The next person was my neighbor who stopped by to tell us they were moving and to say that they would like to take us out for supper. Yes, we would be glad to go out with them. The problem was that we stood at the door to set the time because I was busy with other things. Other things that were not nearly as important as she was and is.

How often I have been busy with other things and so have seen people as an unfortunate interruption. Jesus, who was far

busier than I have ever been or will ever be, found time for those who came to Him. How did He manage? He loved them and knew that people are more important than things. Jesus was desirous of doing the will of God 100% of the time. He loved with a pure love because God is love. I will not become more welcoming by setting my mind to becoming more welcoming. It may work to some extent but if my heart is not in it people will see the difference. Just trying harder will not work. Also feeling guilty and beating myself up is not the solution. What I need is to let God's grace take what Jesus knew and fill my heart with them:
 1. love God and man with all your heart
 2. people are more important than things
 3. make the most of the time by loving others

I need to repent of pride and self and be filled with Jesus' love for people. Then God's love can flow from me to those around me to His glory and honor.

Prayer: Father forgive me for feeling that people are an interruption. I know in my head that You love them as much as You love me and that You have sent them to me to be loved and welcomed even if my time is limited. Send Your Holy Spirit into my heart to change it into a heart that loves others and sees their importance. Make my house into a home that is full of Your love.

A SINGLE OR A DOUBLE

Which of you, if his son asks for bread, will give him a stone? Or if he asks for a fish, will give him a snake? If you, then, though you are evil, know how to give good gifts to your children, how much more will your Father in heaven give good gifts to those who ask him! Matthew 7:9-11

The other day I was riding the bus when two mothers and daughters got on the bus. Because the bus was already full they had to stand. After a few stops people got off and seats became available. One little girl was facing a single seat that was now empty and was determined to sit in it. Her mother kept trying to tell her that behind her was a double seat where she could sit with her friend. The little girl was not even hearing what her mother was saying. She was too focused on sitting in the seat that was right in front of her. Finally amid cries of, "No, no!" the mother simply picked her up and put her in the double seat by her friend. The two were happy little girls for the rest of the bus ride.

As I watched the little girl on the bus, I kept thinking if only she would stop and listen to her mother or even just turn around and look she would save herself the upset that she was putting herself through. What she could see in front of her was better than standing, but what she didn't notice behind her was even better because she could not only sit but could enjoy her friend as well. Many times, I am the little girl wanting what I can see right in front of me and God is trying to tell me that there is something better if only I will trust Him. God has a plan for my life and He wants the very best for me. I don't always (often) see what that plan is ahead of time. As events unroll before me I make conclusions and decide that this must be what God has for me. What I often see is the single empty seat that is right in front of me. It is the seat that I have been hoping will become available and when it does that is all that I can see and all that I desire. God in His loving way tries to change my focus and show me the better way–the double seat behind me. Because I am so focused on what I want, I can't hear the small still voice of God telling me what is better. It is not that the single seat is bad; it is just that the double seat is better. What I want may not be bad or bad for me; it is not the best and God wants the best for me.

I need to learn to have my focus on God rather than myself. I need to learn to stop telling Him what I want and be quiet so I can hear when He tells me what is best.

Prayer: Father, I am sorry for all of the times that I am so busy telling You what I want that I can't hear Your voice telling me what is best. Rid me of my sinful selfishness so that I can hear Your voice and trust You to know what is best not only for me but for those I love as well. When I refuse to stop and listen, I ask that You pick me up and put me where I need to be. Do not let me settle for less than Your best. Teach me to be thankful even as You change my plans.

WHAT IS GOING ON?

If anyone had walked into the kitchen, they would have had great concerns over what was happening. Beth was doubled up gasping for breath while John was sitting in a chair with tears running down his cheeks. Tim and Elaine were the spectators to these events. Everything was Ok. It was great even. Beth had gotten laughing so hard that she fell off the chair and was gasping for breath between the peels of laughter. John also was laughing to the point of crying. What was the cause of such mirth - nothing in particular just a family having fun together. Although there were a few complaints about muscle aches afterward, everyone was happy. It had succeeded in taking the tension out of a busy day.

A cheerful heart is good medicine, but a crushed spirit dries up the bones. Proverbs 17:22

It amazes me how quickly I forget the truth of Proverbs 17:22. When I have aches and pains I run for the Tylenol or I just endure. A favorite word in Japanese is *gaman*. It means to persevere. It is what all good Japanese are taught to do when things are difficult. Although I am not Japanese, I certainly have learned how to *gaman*. I take pride in not complaining. My children say that I don't need to complain as my repeated sighs say more than words ever could. Yes, there are times for taking medicine and times for just simply hanging on.

All too often we fail to have a cheerful heart. What is even worse, we feel guilty if we enjoy ourselves and try to make others feel guilty if they are enjoying themselves and we are not. You would think the verse said, "A crushed heart is good medicine, but a joyful spirit dries up the bones." We get life so wrong and then wonder why it is so hard. We not only crush the laughter out of our own life but we work hard at crushing it from those around us as well. As Christians we may not be laughing all of the time but we certainly should have a heart that knows the source of true joy and lets that joy bubble out.

Where does a Christian's joy come from? It comes from knowing that God knows us absolutely yet loves us unconditionally. He has forgiven our sins and has put His Holy Spirit in us that we may forgive others' sins and love them with God's love. God has adopted us and given us freedom in Christ. He is not angry with us anymore. This alone should produce joy deep in our hearts. Our joy also comes from a deep certainty that no matter how badly we mess things up He can fix it. In His grace He can even use it! God does have a plan and that plan is to create Christ in us.

Prayer: Father, don't let me get so caught up in the serious business of doing that I forget the great joy of being Your child. Teach my heart to not only cry from sorrow but to cry tears of joy as well. Thank You for the times when You break through my seriousness and give times of uproarious fun.

The Tapioca Incident

Thou shalt not covet or thou shalt not be greedy

I haven't thought about covetousness much. When I have thought in terms of greed it generally is about other people and large sums of money. I don't think that is what God had in mind though.

In my family we all really like tapioca pudding. A single recipe says it serves 6. I make a double recipe for the four of us. On one occasion I had made the normal amount. It was still in the pot but ready for consumption. The kids and I had each taken a small (but not too small) bowlful. We relaxed and enjoyed our special treat. John came down from his office and saw us eating tapioca. Thinking we had each taken all we wanted, he proceeded to eat the remaining tapioca. As a group we rose up and accused him of eating our portion and of being greedy. Perhaps he was but so were we. We wanted more for ourselves and were unconcerned for our critical and judgmental spirits toward John. (I now divide the tapioca into 4 equal portions to avoid any further problems.)

Greed can show itself as wanting more money or more possessions or something that is not ours to have (thou shalt not covet they neighbor's wife). Greed can also show itself in desiring to have our rights. In our case it was the right to our share of the pudding. When our greed is not satisfied it can produce disappointment, depression, anger, envy, revenge, hatred, a critical and judgmental attitude and more greed. (Greed is self-reproducing. If you get what you want, it produces more greed. If you don't get what you want it can produce more greed.)

Being thankful for all that God has given us produces joy and peace and a desire to share. Instead of trying to pick the largest bowl, thanksgiving lets us take the smallest bowl–not so we look good and feel good but so that others are blessed to an even greater extent. (It can also be a great diet tool!)

What causes fights and quarrels among you? Don't they come from your desires that battle within you? You want something but don't get it. You kill and covet, but you cannot have what you want. You quarrel and fight. You do not have, because you do not ask God. When you ask, you do not receive, because you ask with wrong motives, that you may spend what you get on your pleasures. James 4:1-3

James eloquently points out that the issue is not whether we have or we don't have. It is the motive–the heart desire that is the real problem. We desire pleasure rather than godliness. When our hearts long for blessings from God rather than for the God of blessing Himself, we are saying that God is not enough; His supreme gifts of love, forgiveness and acceptance are not enough to satisfy. A heart that is focused on receiving has lost sight of the Giver of all good gifts. No wonder God said that we are not to covet. When we do, our hearts become bound to that object or person rather than being fully attached to God.

Prayer: Show me my heart idols and their inability to truly satisfy. May my desire always be for You the Creator rather than for your creation. Fill my heart with an abundance of love for You.

GRANDPA'S LAP

My soul finds rest in God alone; my salvation comes from him.
Psalm 62:1

He who dwells in the shelter of the Most High will rest in the shadow of the Almighty. Psalm 91:1

When I was a little girl my grandfather lived with us. He was a very special person in my life. When I would come home from school, I would climb onto his lap as he sat in his favorite chair. He would talk to me and let me read my first grade books to him. He never looked bored at listening to, "See Spot run." My desire to spend time with him was such that I would convince my teacher at school that I was sick and needed to go home. After my great sick act, I would skip my way home knowing that Grandpa would be there. I did learn that I had to play sick after lunch because if I played sick before lunch Grandpa would send me back to school at lunchtime. This was embarrassing because the teacher would discover that I wasn't really sick. Of course Grandpa knew that I wasn't sick, but my desire to be with him outweighed anything else. It has been years and years since I was in first grade but it still brings a warm comfort to my heart to think of Grandpa. I loved him and enjoyed spending time with him. My goal was not to practice reading but to enjoy the relationship.

When I come to my heavenly Father, I need to have this same desire to enjoy God's company. How often do I come to God with a list of things that I want Him to do in me, for me or for others? Of course it is good to bring all of these things to my heavenly Father. It is good to seek His will and His help. But if the only reason I come to God is for the things He can do, I have lost that which is truly of value–the relationship.

I am far from God's perfect holiness, yet God desires to have fellowship with me because He loves me and sees me as credited with Christ's righteousness. The more I realize the immensity of God's love for me, the more I will desire to spend time simply enjoying that love. My goal will change from desiring something from God to desiring God Himself. Just as I desired to spend time with my grandfather because I loved him so much, even more so I want to worship my heavenly Father from a heart filled with love.

Prayer: Father, help me focus on Your love for me so that my heart will be filled with love rather than thinking only of the things that You can do for me. I thank You that You give great blessings, but teach me to realize more and more that the greatest blessing is knowing You and being loved by You. Never let me take Your love for granted but let me rejoice and rest in Your love each moment of each day.

SHALL WE DANCE?

Let them praise his name with dancing and make music to him with tambourine and harp. For the Lord takes delight in his people; Psalm 149:3-4a

When I was in college I took a ballroom dance class in which I learned to waltz. Like most people, I learned to dance by counting the beats and moving my feet to the appropriate number. The learning process is usually slow but with practice you learn to dance regular speed. You start out 1…2…3…1…2…3 then 1..2..3..1..2..3 and finally 1.2.3.1.2.3. At first, the dance seems not only slow but also unnatural and takes a great deal of concentration. As you improve it becomes fun and is something you look forward to doing on a regular basis.

    Learning to live in the Gospel is much the same. You start out slow but with practice you learn to enjoy what God brings your way. Instead of 1.2.3 it is Repent…Believe…Obey…Repent..Believe..Obey..Repent.Believe.Obey. The Holy Spirit works in your heart to teach you the joy that is yours in Christ. With practice repenting is no longer something to be avoided, but rather becomes something to be sought because it leads you back to Christ. Believing becomes easier because your thoughts are centered on Christ who is the One in whom you believe. After some practice obeying is no longer a grit your teeth and try harder duty but is a loving response to God who loves you. As you practice these steps they get easier and easier not because you ignore your sin but because you know God more and more and experience the love and forgiveness He has for you, so you repent, believe, and obey.

If we try to change the steps, we also change the dance. A waltz that is 1.2.1.2. is no longer a waltz. Just as obey.obey.obey. is not the Gospel, so repent.obey.repent.obey. and believe.believe.believe are also not the Gospel. We need to have all of the steps, in the right order, and with the right motivation in order to dance the Gospel dance. God intends for us to have a life of joy in Christ, not a life of trying and despair. You may waltz to various pieces of music, some cheerier than others. The circumstances in our lives may sometimes be cheery and sometimes be very hard, but if we focus on the Gospel, the Holy Spirit can take us through whatever comes with joy. We will have an increasing awareness of God's grace, His forgiveness, His acceptance, and the delight that He takes in us. We can then delight in our heavenly Father as we repent, believe, and obey.

Are you dancing the Gospel dance? If so, who is your partner and who is leading?

You turned my wailing into dancing; you removed my sackcloth and clothed me with joy, that my heart may sing to you and not be silent. O Lord my God, I will give you thanks forever. Psalm 30:11,12

Prayer: Father, teach me the joy of repenting, believing and obeying but also teach me to do all of these things out of love for you. Never let me think that any of them will make me more acceptable to You or failing to do them well makes me any less loved by You. Let my life be an expression of love coming from You and returning to You. Teach my heart to dance in You alone.

KNOTS

And we know that in all things God works for the good of those who love him, who have been called according to his purpose. Romans 8:28

A couple of years ago a friend of mine stayed up late one night to teach me to tat. For those of you who do not know what tatting is; it is a form of lace making using tiny knots in fine thread to make intricate dainty patterns. My mother used to tat and made gorgeous lace. She always made it look so easy as she would hardly look at what she was doing. This friend also made it seem easy and very learnable. For me it is not that easy and I'm not sure that it is learnable. She would slowly show me how to make the knot and then the all-important step of tightening the knot in the right way in the right place. When I tried I did get knots, just not beautiful knots all tiny and organized. Mine looked more like a 2-year-old who has played in her mother's thread. I was told not to be discouraged, as practice would make great improvements. I must admit that my efforts still look like a 2-year-old's playtime. (I'm stubborn though and I haven't given up yet.)

My life sometimes seems like a series of knots. When God is in charge, all of the knots work together to form a beautiful life that can bring glory to Him. According to Jeremiah 29:11 ("For I know the plans I have for you," declares the Lord, "plans to prosper you and not to harm you, plans to give you hope and a future."), God has a design for my life. Just as someone making lace needs a plan in order to create a beautiful finished work, so God has a plan that will create a beautiful finished work in my life. When I try to be in charge, the knots are just knots and the design is just a jumbled mess. Circumstances seem so incomprehensible and over-whelming. Even little things can become problems. Years of practice at running my life have not improved my abilities. I need to leave that to the Master who can make even the most confusing of times into beauty. Unfortunately I am stubborn and I haven't given up yet. I still think that practice makes perfect and I can handle things this time. I need to learn that no matter how much I practice running my life I can't make it perfect. I need to accept that God has a perfect plan for my life and the expertise to bring about that plan. God is God! He created me and He will perfect me. I am His workmanship! (Ephesians 2:10)

Prayer: Father, forgive me for trying to be in charge and take Your place. Teach my heart to enjoy what You create both in me and around me. I know that You are the Master planner and have a design for my life. I lay aside my own plan and choose Yours instead. Give me faith to believe that You are able and that Your ways are good and kind. Convince my heart that You and You alone are sufficient.

THE WHOLE EARTH SHALL PRAISE HIS NAME

Praise the Lord, O my soul. O Lord my God, you are very great; you are clothed with splendor and majesty. Psalm 104:1

The beauty of nature has always drawn me to it. Perhaps because I live in a huge city, I have come to cherish the times when I can be surrounded by God's creation rather than man's creation. Recently I went to Hokkaido, the most northern of the major islands of Japan. It was a beautiful fall day with the trees changing from green to yellows, oranges, and reds. The mountains rise above the ocean and the birds rose into the air. As I looked at the mountain ranges that slowly faded in hue into the distance, I was reminded of the infinite God who created them. God didn't have to make the mountains so beautiful or make the leaves change color. He could have made the leaves to simply fall off the trees in the fall. It pleased God to create beauty, even beauty that changes with the seasons.

Nature is just a small reflection of God's splendor and majesty. This is a world that has been tainted by man's fall into sin. Can you imagine what the world was like when God created it? How utterly, breathtakingly beautiful it must have been. Now take the next step and think how much more majestic God himself must be, for He is untarnished by sin. We are overwhelmed by creation that is just a small glimpse of the Creator.

We know that the whole creation has been groaning as in the pains of childbirth right up to the present time. Not only so, but we ourselves, who have the firstfruits of the Spirit, groan inwardly as we wait eagerly for our adoption as sons, the redemption of our bodies. Romans 8:22-23

If nature as seen in majestic mountains and gloriously colored leaves is a celebration of God's glory, then how much more should we, His created and redeemed children, be a celebration of praise to Him. Take time today (and everyday) to lift praises to God. Don't let the fall trees outdo our praises. Let us become a people so much in awe and love of God that we can't help but glorify Him who is worthy.

Sing to the Lord, all the earth; proclaim his salvation day after day. Declare his glory among the nations, his marvelous deeds among all peoples. For great is the Lord and most worthy of praise; I Chronicles 16:23-25a

Prayer: Lord, teach my heart to sing Your praises day after day. Forgive me for all of the times when I am more concerned for my glory than for Yours. Let my life become a celebration of You. A celebration not just for what You have done and will do, but a great celebration of who You are–the most high God full of splendor and majesty.

ON THE WINGS OF EAGLES

Even youths grow tired and weary, and young men stumble and fall; But those who hope in the Lord will renew their strength. They will soar on wings like eagles; they will run and not grow weary, they will walk and not be faint. Isaiah 40:30-31

I have never been in a glider or done any hang gliding. I have never even thought about someday wanting to do anything so daring as hang gliding. I am a very feet-on-the-ground kind of person. Because of this earthly orientation, I have never really understood this passage of soaring on wings like eagles. To me this is way over the edge.

Yesterday I was listening to music and watching visual graphics on my computer. The graphics so reminded me of eagles soaring. They were riding the currents and dipping and rising with amazing grace. Along with this the music soared and glided. I had an unbelievable desire to go hang gliding, to see God's creation as an eagle sees it, to feel the air flow around me. If someone had invited me to go hang gliding right then and there, I probably would have. No one did, so true to my earthbound nature, I went for a walk.

I don't think this passage was written with hang gliding in mind though. At the same time that I experienced a desire to hang glide, I also experienced an amazing spiritual and emotional exhilaration. As I physically walked my spirit soared. I felt that trusting God to take me through the currents of life would be the most exiting way to live–the only way to live. When an eagle soars, he does so because it is natural for him. God wants me to spiritually soar with Him because God created me in His image. When Adam and Eve sinned they lost their spiritual wings. Their spirits became earthbound. Jesus died to give me spiritual life. My body is still earthbound but He has given me His Holy Spirit to teach my spirit to soar with Him. I can trust God to hold me up in good weather and in bad (in good circumstances and in bad). My soaring spirit comes not from my circumstances and not from myself but from realizing the tremendous sacrifice of Jesus. This thought lifts my feet off the ground and lets me soar.

Prayer: Lord, take away my feet of fear and give me wings to soar. Teach me the joy of giving you control. Teach my heart to trust in you completely – when the ground is below my feet and when it is not.

THE FRESHNESS OF SPRING

But blessed is the man who trusts in the Lord,
Whose confidence is in him.
He will be like a tree planted by the water
That sends out its roots by the stream.
It does not fear when heat comes;
Its leaves are always green.
It has no worries in a year of drought
And never fails to bear fruit. Jeremiah 17:7-8

Have you ever noticed fresh spring leaves on trees? The brown trees of winter become pale green and alive. Instead of the day-to-day barrenness, they are fresh and alive. They vibrate with a newness and purity that is missing all winter. Seeing spring leaves brings a strange yearning to my heart; a yearning for something more and something less in my life–something more of God and something less of me.

My everyday life can very easily become like a winter tree. It is present but missing the show of life that the leaves give a tree. My life has activity but it is easy for me to miss the inner glow that comes from God. Seeing spring leaves on the trees makes me realize how much more I need God to work in my life. Just as a tree needs the sap to run again in order to give life to new leaves, I need the Holy Spirit to flow in my life and bring forth His fruit.

Life before glory can be like a tree in winter. It has shape and form and usefulness but it is intended to have so much more. My life is often useful but God wants so much more. He wants to produce life not just activity. He wants to produce love not just existence. Just as the new leaves of spring come from within, so this life and love of God come from within. It is the Holy Spirit at work in my heart showing me not only the great love that He has for me and the sacrifice of His Son for my forgiveness but also giving me Jesus' righteousness and adopting me into His family that produces the outward signs of life.

How amazing that from a barren tree can come such freshness and life. How much more amazing that from a sinner, God can produce life and love. Many Christians live much of their life as a winter tree. For many years I was a winter Christian. I had spiritual existence in that I believed in Jesus but I was missing an understanding of my position as a daughter of my Heavenly Father. Praise God that spring can come to a Christian's life no matter what season it is outside. It can always be spring inside as I experience more of the Father's incredible love. It is the security I have in His love that lets me face my sins, turn from them and again let faith lead me to greater obedience and love. May I always let God produce fresh leaves of spring, a newness of life, and a freshness of love for God and for others.

He is like a tree planted by streams of water, which yields its fruit in season And whose leaf does not wither. Whatever he does prospers.
Psalm 1:3

Prayer: Father, let my heart ever be filled with a fresh and growing love for You. Never let me be content with just knowing about You but let Your Holy Spirit produce true life in my heart.

TO WATER OR NOT TO WATER

You will be like a well-watered garden, like a spring whose waters never fail. Isaiah 58:11b

Over the years I have been given many lovely plants. In my ineptitude I have tried three different watering methods. One method was to water and water and water. I discovered that plants die if they are drowned. This is like works alone. Working and working and working will not produce salvation or sanctification anymore than diligent watering of plants will produce growth.

I have also tried the opposite. I have not watered my plants trusting that they would flourish somehow. To no ones surprise, except maybe mine, the plants died. Faith without works is dead. Hoping my plants would grow did not produce growth. In the same way faith in God without good deeds does not produce spiritual growth.

My final method with my plants was to water them once a week. It may not be the best plan for each plant but they have grown. If we truly have faith in Christ, it will show itself in our deeds. Our motive for these deeds is not to earn our way to God nor is it an attempt to get God to do what we want. It is not to get others to think well of us nor to think well of ourselves. But rather our good deeds will come out of a heart filled with His love and grace. This in turn produces faith, love, joy, and obedience in our hearts.

People try to reach God on their own merit, their own good works. Some feel that they come very close or may even reach God by their own deeds. The saddest part is that the very fact of all of their own efforts and their own righteousness show how they fall short of God. Romans 3:10 tells us that "There are none righteous, no not one." God says that it is only through faith that we can please God. Our good deeds done to earn our way to God, only prove how much we need God.

Amazingly, the opposite, faith without good works, is just as mistaken. James tells us that faith without works is dead. How can this be? Faith that is truly faith will produce the works of faith. They are the outward working of the Holy Spirit. So if works without faith do not reach God and faith without works does not please God, what does?

Proper watering will produce growth. Growth will never produce water. Faith produces love and obedience. Obedience will never produce faith. Obedience is a result of faith. If faith has no works, then it is not real faith. If works are not based in faith then they are works of man and not works of God.

Prayer: Father, water my heart and cause it to grow strong in the awareness of Your grace for I know that out of this will grow the flowers of obedience and love. Don't ever let me give in to my pride by trying to produce good deeds on my own. Teach my heart to love You, knowing that out of that love will come joyous determination to live an obedient life for Your glory.

BAD ATTITUDE

The Lord is slow to anger, abounding in love and forgiving sin and rebellion. Numbers 14:18a

We have a turtle named BA (Bad Attitude). His goal in life seems to be to escape from his tank. He stands on his back feet and tries to pull himself over the edge. Most of the time he falls back into the water with a splash but once in a rare while he actually does manage to get out. One time he was sitting next to the tank like a rock. It was like he was saying, "You can't see me because I am camouflaged." If he had been surrounded by rocks, this might have been a good hiding strategy but he was sitting on a white shelf. He definitely stood out. We just picked him up and put him back in the tank. Another time he managed to not only get out of the tank but fall from the cabinet that the tank is sitting on. It is a fall of about 3 feet. We found him banging against the front door with blood on his nose. We put him in a dry tank to make sure that the bleeding stopped and he was OK. He looked so pathetic. "I get hurt and then you punish me. It isn't fair." What wouldn't be fair is to let our turtle escape. You see he has an eating disorder that is not a problem as long as he is being fed by us humans. He would quickly starve if he were on his own in the wild. His problem is that he will only eat turtle food and only one kind at that. One-year mosquitoes laid eggs in his tank and he had the opportunity to eat nice fresh mosquito larvae but he would not. As good pet owners we give him what is best for him even if he does not recognize it as best. Occasionally we let him out for a good run but he always goes back in the tank in the end.

As God's child I could be given the name BA (Bad Attitude). How many times do I rebel against what God gives me? I complain and try to take matters into my own hands and make them work the way I want. I don't believe that God has my best interests at heart but rather that I know what is best for me. I have done this so very many times. Once in a while I do this in a larger matter, but usually it is in what I consider to be small things. The problem is that these small things not only are not what God wants for me but show an inner heart of rebellion. It is my "bad attitude", my unbelief in God's grace where my heart of rebellion is the real problem. God not only desires to take care of me but He is able to do so in ways that greatly surpass my understanding. My heart problems not only prevent me from graciously receiving all that God wants to give me, they also prevent me from having the loving relationship that God desires to have with His children. May God change my rebellious heart and yours as well.

This is what the Sovereign Lord, the Holy One of Israel, says: "In repentance and rest is your salvation, in quietness and trust is your strength, but you would have none of it." Isaiah 30:15

Prayer: Father in Heaven who loves me and desires the very best for me, I ask that You change the name on my heart from "Bad Attitude" to "Believing Child". Because I don't always recognize the rebellion that is in my heart, I ask that You show me my heart and lead me to repentance. Then fill the void with Your love and faith. Teach me to live in contentment rather than in quiet rebellion.

THE GARDEN
Dear children, keep yourselves from idols. I John 5:21

I am not noted as a gardener. Not in the least. Occasionally I have been known to pull weeds. On one occasion I vividly remember pulling weeds that had roots that ran underground for a distance. These roots would then put up fresh weeds that appeared to be totally unconnected. When I would pull one weed, it would lead to another and another. Sometimes (not often) one effort could pull several weeds. At other times the roots would break and I wouldn't even get all of the weed I was pulling.

My heart idols are much like this. God shows me one idol. As I pull out this idol (through repentance and faith) I find that it has roots to another and another. Heart idols have roots that spread to all areas of my life. Two behaviors that seem like completely different weeds share a root idol. These roots are hidden from me but God sees them and wants to show them to me so they can be removed. Just as a weed spreads if it is not dug out, so it is with heart idols. They will grow and spread if we don't let the Great Gardener dig them out.

In my own life I have discovered the weed of fear. If my daughter is late getting home from school, I fear that something awful has happened and she is lying beside the bike path hurt and bleeding. The roots of this weed are attached to the weed of self-centeredness. I'm upset because her being late has caused me to worry. This weed in turn leads to the root of unbelief. I don't trust that God's purposes are best.

My tendency is to want to have ease. Amidst this ease I also want instant progress. Instead of wanting to spend the time and endure the pain of pulling each individual weed, I would like to use a weed whacker. Simply cut the ugly weed off and ignore the root. Make the outside look like change has taken place but no real change has. Just as a weed whacker only works for a very short period to make an area look better, so outward camouflage only hides my heart's weeds for a very, very short time. Even if we cover the weeds with a rug, they are still there putting down more and more roots. We just pretend that they are gone.

I am so thankful that God is the Great Gardener. He does not settle for a garden that simply looks healthy. Rather he works the soil to remove the roots that nourish the weeds. He removes heart idols not just changes our behavior. As a gardener He knows that He has to plant good seeds or the weeds will return. Turning from my heart idols is not enough. I must fill my garden (my heart) with God Himself. When my heart is gripped with the wonder of His greatness, my heart idols lose all of their attraction.

Heart gardening is a two-step process. First remove the weeds, roots and all (repent). Then plant the good seed of the Gospel (believe).

Prayer: Lord, help me to see what my heart longs for by showing me my heart idols. In repentance I turn from them and embrace You. Let the gate to the garden of my heart always be open to You and You alone. Give me eyes to see not only weeds but roots as well. Let my heart be so enthralled with You that my heart's garden is filled with faith in Christ. Be the Great Gardener in my heart, today and always.

A Lamp Unto My Feet

Your word is a lamp to my feet and a light for my path. Psalm 119:105

During the summer we go tent camping at a lake near Mt. Fuji. Unlike Tokyo the mountains get very dark at night. I tend to be night blind so like most people I take along a flashlight. Its light lets me see the path to the bathroom without tripping over tree roots or tent ropes.

There is an interesting difference between a flashlight and a lamp. A flashlight shines only where it is pointed. A lamp shines in all directions. God's Word is a lamp to my feet. Yes, His Word lights my path so that I can avoid the dangers and pitfalls that may lie in front of me. But unlike a flashlight, God's Word is not just directed to my feet. God's Word shines all around. It shines in the dark to show me the way I should go and it shines on me to show me the darkness that is inside me.

I would much rather God show me the path I should follow than show me my heart. I prefer that God's Word was a flashlight that just shone in front of me. It is safe and secure to let God show me the way. It is not so comfortable to stand in the light of God's lamp. I want it to shine out to other people's hearts but not on mine. God loves me and knows me, so He has made His Word into a lamp that will not only direct me in the way I should go, but will also teach me how to trust the One who has kept His promises. Following Jesus is not just about doing the right things in the right places (following the path). It is about being the person God created me to be (having the heart of Christ). Only God who created you and me can change us into the likeness of Christ.

If we insist that God's Word be only a directional beacon, we will find that our Christian path is impossible to walk. Yes, we need a directional beacon because we get lost among the trees of life. The problem is that just knowing the way we should go is not enough. If that were all that we needed then following God would be easy. God gave the Israelites clear directions as to how they should live. They failed miserably. Jesus simplified those instructions into, "Love the Lord your God with all your heart and with all your soul and with all your mind…. And Love your neighbor as yourself." This too is impossible for us. God knows us and loves us yet we don't love Him as we should. As far as loving our neighbor as ourselves, this is totally impossible as our neighbor is not always loveable. (Remember that you are somebody's neighbor.) God created us to be like Jesus and the Holy Spirit is working to make that a reality. For this to happen we need to let the light shine into our hearts. We need to face the sin that it reveals and repent of it. We then need to let God not only cleanse us but to create His image in us.

This is the verdict: Light has come into the world, but men loved darkness instead of light because their deeds were evil. Everyone who does evil hates the light, and will not come into the light for fear that his deeds will be exposed. But whoever lives by the truth comes into the light, so that it may be seen plainly that what he has done has been done through God. John 3:19-21

Prayer: Lord, shine Your light not only on my path but into my heart as well. I may think that I can follow Your path on my own strength but I cannot. I need You to not only lead and guide but also to change me into the person You created me to be. I give You permission to do in me what needs to be done. Let Your light shine in me and through me.

Archaeology

But encourage one another daily, as long as it is called Today, so that none of you may be hardened by sin's deceitfulness. We have come to share in Christ if we hold firmly till the end the confidence we had at first. Hebrews 3:13-14

Archaeologists study cultures that flourished but are long gone. They dig through ruins that have been buried under years and years of accumulated dirt. They find treasures that have long been hidden and bring them to light.

For years when I was asked to share something about my spiritual growth, I always shared about how I became a Christian. Granted it was a miraculous conversion but it soon became an archaeological site. If asked to share something that God did or something spiritual that I learned in the past week or month or year, I was stuck. (I did fake it well though.) It seemed the only spiritual treasures I had were from the past.

Is your Christian life the site of an archaeological dig? Did your faith flourish for a time but now it seems like something from your past? When asked to share something you have learned from God, do you have to look back years to find something to share? If your answer was yes to any of these questions then you are an archaeological Christian.

Praise God that He does not want archaeological children. Yes, He does want us to remember the past but He also wants to work in our hearts and lives in the present. His work was not completed when we became Christians. He worked in our hearts to lead us to Christ and He continues to work in our hearts to lead us in Christ. The same faith that led us to Christ will carry us along with Christ. Colossians 2:6,7 "So then, just as you received Christ Jesus as Lord, continue to live in him, rooted and built up in him strengthened in the faith as you were taught, and overflowing with thankfulness."

I became an archaeological Christian because I forgot that today's life was to be lived by faith. My self-effort slowly but progressively took the place of faith. I tried to live my Christian life on my own strength and thus show God how good I was. The more I did this the dryer my spiritual life became. My faith was buried under layers of self-effort. God did not leave it buried but removed the sediment, revitalized my faith, and brought me back to my first love by reminding me of how much He loves me, showing me how sinful I still am, reminding me of His great forgiveness, and teaching me my position in Christ. He continues to renew me daily, moment by moment.

Today are you a Christian archaeologist digging for spiritual blessings in the past? If so, ask Jesus for His renewal and reformation. Jesus came not just to give us eternal life but also to give us life to the full each and every day and throughout eternity.

Prayer: Father, never let me forget all of the wonderful things that You have done in the past, but don't let me live my life there. Continually teach my heart to rely on You for today, to see You at work all around me, and to trust You for the future. Keep the treasure of faith bright and shiny in my life; don't let me bury it in the past. Keep reviving my love for You so that it does not get old and cold. Thank You that through Your grace I can see that You are always for me and desire the best for me today and always.

THE STENCH OF SIN

Have mercy on me, O God, according to your unfailing love; according to your great compassion blot out my transgressions. Wash away all my iniquity and cleanse me from my sin. Cleanse me with hyssop, and I will be clean; wash me, and I will be whiter than snow. Let me hear joy and gladness; let the bones you have crushed rejoice. Create in me a pure heart, O God, and renew a steadfast spirit within me. Do not cast me from your presence or take your Holy Spirit from me. Restore to me the joy of your salvation and grant me a willing spirit, to sustain me. Psalm 51:1-2, 7-8, 10-12

A while ago I was going downtown Tokyo and since I don't drive, I was taking the train. I am one of those people who always look for a seat. I don't push and shove but I really do like having a seat. The train I got on had a few people standing but I did spot one empty seat. Without a second thought I sat and discovered why no one else was sitting in that seat. I had just sat next to the worst stench that I had ever smelled. It was a combination of unwashed person and urine and who knows what else. I no longer wanted to sit in this seat, but I also didn't want to offend this man. He may have stunk and been homeless but he was still a person and had feelings. He may not even have realized how badly he smelled to those around him. My perhaps cowardly but at least not totally unkind solution was to get off the train at the next stop and move to a different car of the same train.

    I haven't thought about this experience for quite some time. I was reading about man's (my) sinful condition in comparison to God's holiness when this incident came to mind. In God's view I am the homeless man who stinks. His is a physical condition that can easily be improved by clean clothes and a bath. I had a very limited compassion for the homeless man. I did not offer any help for his problem(s) but I did try to not add to them. My spiritual condition is not so easily dealt with. Perhaps the hardest part of this process is to admit that in God's sight my sins are more offensive than the smell of that homeless man. His condition was a surface one where mine is internal and deeply rooted. God in His infinite love and mercy has provided a solution to my problem of sin. He sent His only Son to die in my place for the forgiveness of my sins. God then offers me this great gift free of charge. But God does not stop there. He also has sent His Holy Spirit to live in me and continue the cleansing process.

This cleansing is ongoing. For the homeless man a bath will help the immediate problem. But one bath and then no more will not solve the problem in the long run. Bathing must become a way of life for it to have continuous effects. The same is true for you and me. Our spiritual cleansing must be an ongoing process, not just a one-time act. The Holy Spirit does this by showing us our sin and then leading us in repentance to the cross of Christ for the forgiveness and cleansing that we so desperately need.

Prayer: Loving Father, I am so thankful that You do not love me based on who I am or what I do but that You love me based on Christ, Your own Son. Let me take the words of Psalm 51 to heart and not just to mind. Lead me in the way of repentance and cleanse my inner being today and each day that I might come to reflect Jesus, my Savior and Lord.

A Wild Goose Chase

May our Lord Jesus Christ himself and God our Father, who loved us and by his grace gave us eternal encouragement and good hope, encourage your hearts and strengthen you in every good deed and word.
2 Thessalonians 2:16-17

The other day I decided to go downtown Tokyo to run some errands. I wanted to go to the used English bookstore and I needed to go to another bookstore to get English conversation textbooks. I packed up the books I wanted to exchange and off I went. I got to the used bookstore with no problems only to find out that Wednesday they do not exchange books. They did let me leave the books and said that I could come back another day.

In my rush to get to the next bookstore, I quickly jumped on a train. When the train pulled out it went the wrong way. I told myself not to panic; I would simply get off at the next stop and get on the right train. They then announced that the next stop was Yokohama a 25-minute train ride. My first reaction was to mentally beat myself up for being so stupid as to not read the sign before hurriedly jumping on a train. Since I didn't have a book with me to read I had lots of time to preach the Gospel to myself. Jumping on the wrong train was not a sin and I did not need to feel guilty about making a mistake. Wrong train or right train makes no difference in how God loves me and is with me. I could enjoy spending this extra time focused on God and His grace in my life, or I could sit on that train and be miserable. On this occasion I chose to spend the time enjoying God. An hour later I got to the textbook store only to discover that it was closed on Wednesday. The "goose" may have gotten away but I learned a valuable lesson about enjoying God no matter what the day brings.

How is your day? Are you accomplishing all that you set out to do or is the "goose" getting away from you? No matter how your day is going, you can choose to enjoy God's presence in your life. He will never leave you and He will always love you with a perfect love. He knows the stupid things you do, the sinful things you do, and the good things you do and loves you for today and for eternity! If today is a "stupid" day for you, remember that God loves you. If today is a sinful day, repent of your sin, believe the Gospel and remember that God loves you. If today is a good day, be thankful for His grace and remember that God loves you. There probably is a "wild goose chase" day coming and God will spend it with you.

Prayer: Father, never let me forget how much You love me not based on how good or how bad I am but based on Your provision thru Christ. Thank You for sacrificing Your Son so that I might know Your great love and forgiveness. Let my heart always be warmed by Your love and let me share that love with those around me.

Right in Their Own Eyes

Every way of a man is right in his own eyes: but the Lord pondereth the heart. KJV Proverbs 21:2

There is a way that seems right to a man, but in the end it leads to death. Proverbs 14:12

I like to be right. That is an understatement. I really love to be right all of the time. I have been known to nag my husband and harass my children to get them to do whatever it is that I am sure is the right thing. This is not a recommended method even on those occasions when I am right. But it is really bad on all of those occasions when I am wrong. My problem is that I am so sure that I am right that the needs and wishes of others are not important. These issues are not ones that are spelled out in the Scriptures. I know that you shall not kill or lie or steal. Scripture does not say anything about going to bed at 10:00 or getting a haircut. The Bible does say that I am to love others. I especially need to love my family. When I do what is right in my own sight, I usually break the command to love one another.

It may not be as obvious but it is just as true that I also break the command to love God with all of my heart and mind and soul when I am determined to be right. Loving myself becomes the main focus of my attention. God is pushed into some corner where it is easy to ignore Him. Fortunately for me and those around me, God does not like to be ignored and always manages to get my attention. His goals are always right and His method is always loving.

Proverbs makes it clear that our ways are not God's way. Our ways will not only lead to miscommunication but death of the relationship. This is true of our relationships with family and friends and is also true of our relationship with God. I am fortunate that my family has not stopped speaking to me or loving me because of my desire to be right. It has at times distanced relationships and caused unnecessary tension. Although God chooses to love me even when I am rebellious to Him, my rebellious desire to be right does move me outside of God's perfect will for my life.

I need to repent of my own self-rightness and accept God's rightness that He offers through faith in His Son, Jesus. This allows me to love God and others and amazingly it allows me to love myself as God loves me. I no longer have to be right in order to feel good about who I am. I am found righteous in Christ and am loved not based on my rightness but on Christ's. Those around me can then be loved not based on their performance. And most of all I can love God out of a heart that is being changed into the likeness of Christ.

Prayer: Father, forgive me for all of the times that I have been more interested in establishing my own rightness than in resting in Christ's. Change my heart from one of self-centered rightness to one that loves as You love. Take the relationships that I have damaged and heal them out of Your love. May You be glorified through my life.

UNSPEAKABLE JOY
You will be like a well-watered garden, like a spring whose waters never fail. Isaiah 58:11b

Well-spring of the joy of living, Ocean depth of happy rest
Joyful music lifts us sunward in the triumph song of life
                from *Joyful, Joyful, We Adore Thee* by Henry van Dyke

Today it is raining! Yesterday it was raining! Tomorrow it will probably be raining! This is rainy season in Japan. It often lasts from mid-June to mid-July. Usually I have a hard time staying cheery and upbeat during rainy season. Today is amazing though. The cool air and the sound of the gentle rain seem to fill me with a wonder for the great blessings of God.

    Just outside my window is a large cherry tree. Because it is so large all I can see are the branches and the green leaves. It is almost like living in my own woods in the midst of the city. The leaves are bright green and glistening with drops of water. There is no sunshine flashing its rays on them but that is OK. They don't need the sunshine to be beautiful. The raindrops give a glistening life to the leaves and then continue on to the soil below. God creates beauty even on rainy days. This beauty is there for all to see if they will only take the time to stop and notice.

    In my life there are days and weeks and sometimes months

and years that seem far from beautiful. Sometimes it is circumstances that seem to drag me down. More often it is my preoccupation with my busy-ness that keeps me from experiencing a deep relationship with God. As my relationship cools, so does the joy of my salvation. I cannot see all of the blessings that surround me. It is as though my life becomes rainy season.

Today I'm learning to see the beauty of rainy season. It doesn't make the rain turn to sunshine but it does make the dreariness turn to joy. When I'm in the middle of difficult circumstances, seeing God's blessings may not make the circumstances change. I will be changed instead. I can experience God's joy and peace. As I return God's joy to Him in a heart full of joy, it will lift me to the Father so that I can see the triumph that is mine in Christ.

> But let all who take refuge in you be glad;
> Let them ever sing for joy.
> Spread your protection over them,
> That those who love your name may rejoice in you.
>
> Psalm 5: 11

Prayer: Father, teach me to resist being so busy with life that I miss living in You. Give me eyes to not only see the glisten of water on leaves but to see the blessings that surround me. Give me Your joy so that I can then pass those blessings on to others. Let me ever sing for joy–not based on my circumstances but based on You and Your good intensions for me.

THE BRANCH CUT OFF

Remain in me, and I will remain in you. No branch can bear fruit by itself; it must remain in the vine. Neither can you bear fruit unless you remain in me. John 15:4-5

We were given a beautiful stately rubber plant. The plant flourished except for one branch at the top that was mostly bare. (I know this is hard to believe given my aptitude at killing plants.) In order to make the plant more attractive I cut off the barren branch and set it aside to throw away. The remainder of the plant has grown to the point that after a 7-week absence Beth was not sure that it was the same plant. The cut off branch continued to have green leaves for a short period of time but eventually it turned all brown and was dead.

When we believe in Jesus as our Savior, we are grafted into the family of God. He sends the Holy Spirit to nourish us and grow us into the image of Christ. The secret to spiritual growth is staying attached to the vine, as it says in John 15.

I used to wonder why Jesus had emphasized the importance of staying attached to the vine. As Christians we are grafted on to the vine. I have never had a branch of a plant that of its own volition decided to unattach itself from the plant. A part of the plant is a part of the plant. They belong together. I have always felt that when God attaches someone to His vine they stay attached. If this is the case then why does Jesus exhort believers to stay attached to the vine? In looking back over my Christian experience I have learned an answer to that question.

As a new believer my entire life and thought centered on what Christ had done for me. I felt called to be a missionary and gladly went to the mission field. This is when my attachment problems began to show themselves although it was years before I recognized them for what they were. Somehow I had started to live my Christian life as a way of showing God how good I was so that He would be pleased with me. I tried very hard to be a good Christian but I was drawing from my own resources and not from the vine, Jesus Christ. Because of this I found that I became more and more spiritually dry. My life began to resemble that rubber plant branch that I had cut off. It continued to be green for a while but it could not sustain growth and withered. Because God loves me He did not let me die but He did allow me to wither so that I could see what I had lost. I was trying to live a Christian life without drawing daily nourishment from the source of all life. I still struggle with self-effort and a desire to be in control, but through repentance and faith the Holy Spirit continually leads me back to the cross.

Jesus knew that we have a strong tendency to want to do things on our own. Our motivation may seem good: we want to do good for others, we want to lead others to Christ, or we want to be good Christians. The only way we can accomplish these good things is to stay attached to the vine as Jesus exhorted us to do. Our struggle with this does not go away as we mature in our Christian life. It may even become more of a struggle as spiritual pride adds to the problem. We don't need to focus on the struggle but rather focus on the vine.

Prayer: Father, keep my wandering heart focused solely on You. So often, without even realizing it, I try to do things for You in order to earn Your love and acceptance. Forgive me and help me to realize in ever-deeper ways how much You love and accept me not based on what I do, but based on what Christ has already done for me. Let Your strength be my strength and Your love be my love.

SIN AND THE COMPUTER VIRUS

And I will ask the Father, and he will give you another Counselor to be with you forever–the Spirit of truth. The world cannot accept him, because it neither sees him nor knows him. But you know him, for he lives with you and will be in you. I will not leave you as orphans; I will come to you. John 14:16-18

The other day my husband received an e-mail with an attachment. There is nothing unusual about that but this particular attachment had a computer virus. Fortunately my husband's machine detected the virus and removed it before it got into his machine. He sent a message to the original sender warning him of the virus. As is usually the case the sender was unaware that he had a virus. The sender was then able to download a virus detector and remove the virus from his own machine. As my husband says, computer viruses are just like sin in that they demand constant vigilance and detection. How very true this is.

We live in a day and age when it is easy to get a computer virus and not even be aware of it. Worse still you can be sending that same virus to your friends. There are all kinds of viruses that do all sorts of things to your computer. Fortunately with the right software it is possible to detect these viruses and remove them before they have a chance to do any mischief.

In our spiritual life, sin is like a virus that is waiting for its chance to damage us often in ways that we are not entirely aware of. God has provided a means to detect sin and fight against it by sending the Holy Spirit to dwell in us. Just like computer software that has to be upgraded to fight the latest viruses, the Holy Spirit must be fresh in our lives each day. Christ died on the cross once and we need only receive Him once. But to live a life in Christ takes constant vigilance by the Holy Spirit. We need to be still and allow the Holy Spirit to search our hearts, show us our sin, and bring us to repentance. God's Spirit never tires or rests. He is always working to protect us from the harmful viruses of sin. The problem is that we don't always take advantage of His presence.

On my computer I can choose to receive material that is not checked by my virus scanner. This is not a wise move because viruses often come from people you know without their being aware that they have sent them. In my spiritual life I can choose to ignore the Holy Spirit. I most often do this when I think that everything is fine and I can handle life by myself. I take the place of the Holy Spirit. Just as with a virus scanner that is not used, the damage is done before we even know there is danger.

It is the role of the Holy Spirit to make us into the image of Christ. We are not totally there yet and we won't be until we get to heaven. Each day He works in us to change not only our behavior but also our inner motives and desires. The Holy Spirit is a heart sin detector. When He shows us sins in our hearts we don't need to panic. We can face the sin because we know that God loves us and will not reject us. We can confess the sin, repent of it, and be cleansed from it. Rebecca Manley Pippert in her book *Hope Has Its Reasons* says, "But to experience and benefit from the cure we must turn to him and quit pretending there is nothing wrong with us." In order for a virus protector to protect we must use it. In order for the Holy Spirit to work we must turn to Him and cooperate with Him.

Prayer: Father give me a heart that desires you more than it desires sin. Fill my heart with Your love so that when You show me my sin, I can face it and repent. Don't ever let me be content with yesterday's repentance but through daily repentance form me into the image of Christ Jesus my Savior and Lord.

THE EDDIES OF LIFE

Some trust in chariots and some in horses, but we trust in the name of the Lord our God. They are brought to their knees and fall, but we rise up and stand firm. Psalm 20:7,8

A number of years ago my family went white water rafting. It was a beautiful Wyoming day for rafting. We all were having a great time- just enough excitement without it being too tense. Then came the eddy; a whirlpool that sucks everything in and then keeps it. Our raft was just on the edge of the eddy. I was on the side away from the eddy so I didn't fully understand why we were instructed to paddle with all we had. Since not fully understanding has never stopped me before, I paddled. John was on the other side of the raft and had no problem understanding the need to paddle. He could not only see the eddy but could feel its pull on the raft. We did successfully escape the eddy and continued to enjoy the day. That eddy didn't leave much of an impression with me but John has often spoken of it over the years. We were in the same raft but our experiences were very different.

Life has its share of eddies also. Worry/anxiety is a common whirlpool that can easily suck us in and keep us. We don't have to give in as God has given us His Holy Spirit to not only show us the whirlpools in life, but to then give us the strength we need to paddle away from them.

Yesterday I experienced this first hand. John and Beth left for six weeks in the States. I was feeling sad and lonely but knew that I could adjust. After all, I am a big girl now. In the morning I decided to send them an e-mail. This turned out to be the beginning of the whirlpool but I didn't know it yet. I struggled for about an hour to get the computer set correctly so that the e-mail could be sent. Failure. As a break, I listened to the messages on the answering machine. After several hang-ups, there was a message that said it was from the police and if John did not call, they would arrest him. The whirlpool had me now. Praise God, John called from America soon after this and I was able to explain about the message. He called the police station from America only to find out that they had not left the message and never would leave such a message. John assured me that it was nothing to be concerned about and gave me instructions for the computer. As the day progressed I kept finding myself thinking about the message on the machine. Even though the police assured us that there was no need for concern, I continued to live in the eddy of worry and anxiety. The Holy Spirit finally got through to me that this was not where I wanted to live for the next six weeks. All I had to do was trust Him and I would be free from this terrible trap of worry. It was absolutely amazing. When I did finally trust God, I had peace and contentment for the rest of the day. I even got the e-mail working.

We can't always control the things that come into our lives but we can choose how we will respond to them. When we realize that God is paddling our raft, we can rest in the assurance that He is in control even in the middle of the eddies. On our own strength the circumstances of life will overwhelm us but with God paddling our raft we can have peace in the midst of difficulty.

Prayer: Lord, I thank You that You are desirous of giving me peace when I dwell in You. Help me to continue to trust You even when life seems calm and peaceful. Touch my heart with the beauty of Your voice as it leads and guides me. Let me never take the credit for the things that You do for me and in me. Let me always sing your praises.

THE SMELL OF SMOKE

It is a burnt offering to the Lord, a pleasing aroma, an offering made to the Lord by fire. Exodus 29:18b

For we are to God the aroma of Christ 2 Corinthians 2:15a

When I was growing up in Iowa we, like all of our neighbors, raked leaves in the fall. After the children had had ample time to play in them, they were burned. To this day whenever I smell burning leaves I remember my childhood. It is amazing how certain aromas bring back memories. If the leaves were dry they burned quickly but if we had had rain during the fall the leaves would burn producing a lot of smoke. It is this smoke that I remember smelling. If anyone within several blocks was burning leaves you could smell it. Everyone was very careful to only burn on windless days and to watch their fires to prevent any spread. Today burning leaves is not allowed not only for the danger of fire spreading but also for the pollution from the smoke.

In the Old Testament the Hebrews were instructed by God to make burnt sacrifices. The smoke from the burning was a pleasing aroma to God. Both the Old and New Testaments make it clear that it is not the offering that is most important but rather the heart of the person. (Hosea 6:6 "For I desire mercy, not sacrifice, and acknowledgment of God rather than burnt offerings." Mark 12:33 "To love him with all your heart, with all your understanding and with all your strength, and to love your neighbor as yourself is more important than all burnt offerings and sacrifices.") What God desires is not the offering of animals but rather the offering of our hearts to Him. The Hebrews had a tendency to forget the heart but continue the outward actions. They made the sacrifices that God requested but not out of a heart of love and devotion. We are not that different from the ancient Hebrews. Instead of burning an offering, God wants to set our hearts on fire with love for Him, which then spreads to love for our neighbors. We don't need to fear this kind of fire spreading because when it spreads it brings glory to God rather than destruction. It is the aroma of our hearts burning with love for God that is pleasing to Him.

We can very easily fall into the habit of doing the right things but having our hearts far from God. For example, we go to church but do not worship the true living God. Rather, we worship the god of seeming respectable to others or try to force God to answer our prayers based on our perceived goodness. In Matthew 15:8-9 Jesus says, "These people honor me with their lips, but their hearts are far from me. They worship me in vain; their teachings are but rules taught by men." Let us repent of our self-righteous worship and worship God with hearts that are on fire with love for Him and therefore produce the true aroma of God pleasing sacrifice.

Prayer: Father, send the Holy Spirit to set my heart aflame for You as I see the depth of Your love. Let this love spread through all I do and say and think. Then let it spread to those around me. Help me to look into my own heart and see my motivations. Teach me to repent of all those things that motivate me that are not founded in a deep abiding love for You.

Water For Our Souls

Jesus answered, "Everyone who drinks this water will be thirsty again, but whoever drinks the water I give him will never thirst. Indeed, the water I give him will become in him a spring of water welling up to eternal life." John 4:13-14

Several years ago our family went hiking in the mountains near Mt. Fuji with another family. It was a beautifully clear summer day. As we left our campsite it seemed like a perfect day for a hike–warm but not too warm. By the time we were ready to start hiking it was getting warmer but it was still a fine day. It didn't take long for us to realize that we should have brought something to drink with us. The temperature continued to rise, as did the mountain that we were climbing. The climb consisted of a series of stairs built into the side of the mountain. They were not nice even stairs but made out of logs and dirt. It took us about 2 hours of sweating and complaining and pain to climb those stairs. When we were only about half way up the mountain, the Japanese word for stairway, *kaidan*, became a nasty word.

Added to our ever-growing tiredness from the stairs was an ever-increasing thirst. We finally made it to the top of the mountain and the view was breath-takingly beautiful. Far below us was the lake on which we were camping and behind us was a spectacular view of Mt. Fuji. As wonderful as the view was, it did not solve the problem of our thirst. We continued along the top of the mountain and eventually came to a small store that sold shaved ice with flavored syrup (similar to American snow cones but much better). These were the best *kouri* (snow cones) we had ever eaten. Probably they were about the same as other snow cones but we were so hot and tired and thirsty that they tasted better.

Our Christian life can seem like a never-ending climb up steep stairs. Yes, there are stairs of hard circumstances in the life of a Christian but we do not have to climb them alone and we certainly do not have to be dieing of thirst. Jesus said that He is the water of life and those who come to Him will not be thirsty but will have springs of water flow from them.

There have been times in my Christian life where I have felt like my soul was in the middle of a dry desert with no water in sight. This was not because God had deserted me but because I was foolishly looking in the wrong places for the source of life-giving water. Jeremiah 2:13 "My people have committed two sins: They have forsaken me, the spring of living water, and have dug their own cisterns, broken cisterns that cannot hold water." I had tried to become my own water source. The more I searched for spiritual water the drier I got because I was searching in the wrong places. I was looking to my heart idols to provide that which only God can give. Idols such as job, the approval of others, or self-centered religious devotion can never produce rivers of living water. They promise contentment and satisfaction but they are short lived at best. Heart idols actually make us thirstier for the wrong things.

We need to drink from living water daily and let Christ and Christ alone satisfy the deepest longings of our souls. He is what we are seeking to water our souls.

Prayer: Father, forgive me for all of the times that I have tried to satisfy my soul with things rather than with the true living water found only in Christ Jesus my Lord. Give me this day and every day the refreshing water that brings eternal satisfaction.

MISSION IMPOSSIBLE
Rejoice in the Lord always. I will say it again: Rejoice! Philippians 4:4

How do we rejoice in God? Do we grit our teeth and say, "I will rejoice. I will rejoice." No. Rejoicing comes from the heart not from determination. Does this mean we need to always be in good circumstances in order to feel like rejoicing? No. It says always, not just when you feel like it. So how can this be? I know in my own life there are times when rejoicing is easy and natural and is truly rejoicing. I know there are other times when rejoicing is wooden and forced. If God wants heart felt rejoicing, how can I, an emotional sinner, produce this? I can't do it by sheer will power or determination.

I am learning to translate this verse as "Repent in the Lord always. I will say it again: Repent!" It is through repentance that we draw closer to God. When we live in fellowship with God, we know joy. Rejoicing is natural because no matter how good or how bad our circumstances, we have God's love. Knowing the pure love of God is worth rejoicing about. Our rejoicing must be in the Lord for that is the only place to find true joy.

As I was writing this, God brought me an opportunity to practice what I write. I have been teaching a lot of classes as well as packing Tim's stuff so he can move back to America. Along with this comes the emotion of having to say good-bye. On top of this the people that we have been ministering to at Niiza were all coming on Saturday to supper and for a Bible time. I needed to have something prepared to share from Scripture and food prepared for all of them to eat. Just as I was feeling overwhelmed by all of this, John got a phone call from the pastor of the church where he will speak on Sunday asking if I would share a testimony in Japanese. This was Friday morning and I would be gone most of Friday. John said, "Yes, Elaine would be willing to do that."

Rejoicing at this point seemed like mission impossible. How could I possibly rejoice when life was so overwhelming? As I prayed for God to show me again that I was His daughter and repented of my doubts when things seemed out of my control, the peace of God began to fill my soul. I realized that all of these things are in God's very capable hands. I am able to rejoice in the God of my salvation not based on my performance but based on Jesus and His performance.

I not only got everything done with a joyful heart but on Saturday I was able to go out to lunch with my son. Repentance is truly the way to rejoice!

Prayer: Father, keep my heart repentant. Let my focus always be on You rather than on myself and my abilities. Give me a heart that rejoices not in my accomplishments but in You.

WHITEWATER RAFTING

In God, whose word I praise, in God I trust; I will not be afraid. What can mortal man do to me? Psalm 56:4

Many years ago, John and I went to Wyoming to the Grand Tetons for our honeymoon. As part of our honeymoon package we had a choice between rafting on a slow moving but beautiful part of the Snake River or whitewater rafting on a much rougher part of the river. We chose to go whitewater rafting. It was definitely an exciting ride. At one point a wave of whitewater went over the entire raft. We hung on for dear life. It was truly for "dear life" because the water was so cold that a person who fell in would not have lasted long. No one fell in or was hurt in any way. We simply had an exciting afternoon on the river. Of course there were quiet parts as well. It was during these lulls that we could catch our breath as well as look around and enjoy the wonders of the nature that surrounded us. Among other things we saw a bald eagle in the wild. We have such fond memories that years later we took our children back to the same place and went whitewater rafting with them. They too enjoyed the thrill of riding the rapids.

Just as we had a choice to make of what kind of ride we wanted to take on the river, we have a choice of what kind of ride we want to take with Jesus. We can choose the quiet safe life where we feel that we have a sense of control over what happens to us and in us. Or we can choose to ride the rapids. We no longer think that we are in control. We know that we need the Holy Spirit to be in control because life in all of its wonder is beyond our control.

When I look at my own life, what I see amazes and disappoints me. I chose to ride the rapids of the river and found it to be a thrilling and positive experience. Later I chose to go to Japan as a missionary. Many people would classify this as very daring. Despite these supposedly daring events, I have often chosen to live my life in seeming quietude. For me this quietude is a failure to reach out to others and be vulnerable. I would rather have control than to let God have control. You never know what will come if God is in charge. Around the bend may be rapids that will scare you to death. (Not really it may just seem that way at the time.) Tomorrow God may want to do something so amazing that it will take your breath away. I desperately need the Holy Spirit to teach my heart how to truly trust Him and then let Him sweep me away as He chooses. It is a life that is out of my control. It will not be quiet and peaceful all of the time but it certainly will not be dull. It will bring glory to God my Creator and Father. This is what true living is all about.

Prayer: Lord, show me ways I am not risking but being safe. Teach my heart to trust You in such a way that I am willing to give You full control. Let me give up doing things my way, or the way that seems right to me. Instead let me turn to You that I might see the true way of living. You have said that perfect loves casts out fear. Teach my heart to love You with purity. I know that as I come to know You better and love You better, I will no longer fear what the future may bring whether it be still water or rapids. You are always in the boat and know how to steer it to safety. I don't need to fear because whether You calm the rapids or take me through them, You will always be with me.

TAKE YOUR BREATH AWAY

LORD, I have heard of your fame; I stand in awe of your deeds, O LORD. Renew them in our day, in our time make them known; in wrath remember mercy. Habakkuk 3:2

Today I was listening to a song and the words struck me in a way that they never had before. "…the thought of what could happen takes your breath away." Does the thought of what God could make happen in and through my life take my breath away?

Once in a rare while I see the sun rise from behind the mountains. This always seems to catch me unaware and I watch in awe and wonder. The beauty of nature has an awe inspiring and calming effect on me. Unfortunately, I live in the city and I can't experience nature first hand very often. I am learning to see the small wonders that exist even in the city. Yesterday it rained and some of the raindrops stayed on the just forming buds of the cherry tree outside my window. They sparkled and shone in the sunlight. I can't say that they took my breath away but they did get my attention and draw my thoughts to the One who created them.

The deeper and perhaps harder question is: Does the thought of what God could make happen take my breath away? Do I live in awe and utter amazement at the promises of God? Not nearly as I should. I do recall one time last year when the thought of what God could do literally took my breath away and brought tears to my eyes. John and I were standing in the back of the meeting room where the CPI (Church Planting Institute) Japan Conference had just ended. We had finished packing the last of the boxes and picking up those things that were accidentally left behind by others. John read Habakkuk 1:5. "Look at the nations and watch – and be utterly amazed. For I am going to do something in your days that you would not believe, even if you were told." Our prayers for Japan and the world seemed much too small. God has things that He is going to do that we cannot even imagine. Can you picture Japan as a Christian nation sending missionaries to the far corners of the earth? Can you imagine God pouring out His Spirit on the Japanese people and seeing revival flood this country of stone images and hardened hearts? Do these ideas take your breath away? They certainly take mine away.

Prayer: Lord, teach my heart to be utterly and totally amazed at what You can do. Set my heart on fire afresh. Let my heart burn with a holy blaze that will never burn out but will spread to all of those around me. Start with my dry, hard heart and fill it with wonder at Your power and majesty. Open my eyes to see creation as You see it. Don't let me be so busy getting things done that I miss what You are doing around me and want to do in me.

ELECTIVE SURGERY

You intended to harm me, but God intended it for good to accomplish what is now being done, the saving of many lives. Genesis 50:20

He will wipe every tear from their eyes. There will be no more death or mourning or crying or pain, for the old order of things has passed away. Revelation 21:4

Surgery is a painful experience. Anyone who has had even minor surgery knows how true this statement is. Sometimes we choose to have surgery and sometimes it seems like the surgery chooses us. It doesn't matter who does the choosing, the immediate result is pain. Of course during the surgery we feel no pain due to anesthesia. It is afterward that the pain arrives. Modern medications can deal with a lot of the pain for us and help us to recover faster with fewer complications. Even time is on our side as it erases a lot of the memory of the pain. Years after the surgery all we may have left is better health and a scar or two. Surgeons are even getting good at not leaving scars behind.

God does surgery in our hearts as well. His surgery is always elective in that we must agree that there is a problem and that God's grace is the solution. Even though it seems at times that we go kicking and screaming into surgery, He will never operate without our cooperation. He loves us and always knows what is best for us even when we try to give Him a second opinion. We don't often realize how radical the surgery is that we need but God does. He never does unnecessary surgery and He never cuts deeper than is needed. He even sends His own Holy Spirit to bind up the wounds that He leaves behind.

So why do we deny that we need surgery? We pretend to ourselves, others, and God that we are fine. We think that all we need is a little medicine and the problem will go away. If all we needed was a little medicine, God would not have sent His Son to die for our sins. We need surgery and we need it now. Unfortunately, we think, God does not use anesthesia. We have to be awake for his kind of surgery. His surgery involves showing us our sinfulness, the deep ugly blackness that lives in us, and then not only showing us His great forgiveness but also giving us His own righteousness.

Sometimes God sends us hard circumstances that we don't understand. We don't see the loving hand of the surgeon but only feel the pain of the knife that has cut into our emotions. It is at times like this that we desperately want God to heal the wound but we also need Him to work His righteousness into our hearts. We need to agree to let God do the surgery that is so very essential for our life and well-being. He is the master surgeon and we can trust Him to not only take us through the hard times, but to work wonders in us as well. I think of Joseph who was sold into slavery by his own brothers. Because Joseph went through the surgery that God deemed necessary, later in his life he could say to his brothers that although they meant it to harm him, God meant it for good.

Prayer: Father let me take the pain that I feel and give it to You. All I ask is that You use it for good. Cut out the cancerous growth of sin and replace it with Your perfect righteousness. Let me stay close to You and learn the lessons that You would teach me. I love You and desire to be all that You made me to be.

TREE REMOVAL

The Lord bless you and keep you; the Lord make his face shine upon you and be gracious to you; the Lord turn his face toward you and give you peace. Numbers 6:24-26

Today they cut down the cherry tree in our back yard. We have an extremely small back yard and the tree had grown quite large. It brushed against our house, the neighbor's house, and was headed for a third house. In the fall, it dropped leaves on three yards and the parking lot for the neighboring apartments. Every year I would mumble about the mess that had to be cleaned up. It was not a beautifully shaped tree, which was OK because I hardly ever looked at it except in the spring when it was in bloom. It should have been removed several years earlier but wasn't because we weren't sure how to remove it. Because of all of the close buildings and fences, the removal company brought a crane in order to safely remove it. They did a wonderfully safe and amazingly quiet job. I was in the house and hardly knew it was gone until I looked out the window.

What surprises me is how saddened I am now that the tree is gone. I know that I will enjoy more sunshine this winter but I will certainly miss the Japanese cherry blossoms when spring comes. Sometimes things that are ultimately for the best still cause us sorrow and adjustment. Although these are not pleasant in the short term, they can be very beneficial short and long term. I look out the window and see that the backyard looks so much better and I am glad. Yet at the same time I am saddened at the loss of the tree.

God's work in my life often reminds me of the removal of our cherry tree. I know that what God is doing is for the best. The changes He is making are for my ultimate good and produce results that bring joy and contentment into my life. The problem is that I don't always want to let go of my favorite heart idols. They are comfortable and I have had them for so long that I don't even see them as idols but rather as old friends. When God has pointed them out to me, I know with my head that He is right and they must go. The hard part comes when I remove the idols. It feels like a piece of me has died. It is at this point that I refocus my heart affections to God, my heavenly Father, who loves me enough to give me what is best for me. As I trust Him, He fills my heart with His love, joy and hope. I know that just as the tree removal lets the sunshine into my room, my idol removal lets the Son shine into my heart in a new and wonderful way.

The workmen did a wonderful job of cutting the tree off at ground level. You can hardly tell that there was a tree there only hours ago. Because the roots are still in the ground there is a possibility that shoots may appear. In the same way I have to keep an eye on the areas where God has done heart idol removal. Unfortunately, the roots still produce new growth that needs to be removed before it grows into a great tree.

Prayer: Father, give me the honesty to recognize my heart idols for what they are. Convince me that they are not worthy to even be compared to Your infinite beauty. Teach my heart to seek fulfillment from You alone. Realizing that it may be uncomfortable or hard for a time, I still choose to let go of those things in my life that rob my heart of full devotion to You. Thank You that You have not left me to try to do this on my own but You have sent Your Holy Spirit to dwell in me and guide me.

No "A" Students

This righteousness from God comes through faith in Jesus Christ to all who believe. There is no difference, for all have sinned and fall short of the glory of God, and are justified freely by his grace through the redemption that came by Christ Jesus. Romans 3:22-24

I grew up and went to a typical American public school. Those who did really well on the tests got A's. Those who did well got B's. Those who did OK got C's. Those who did poorly got D's and those who did really poorly got F's. Your sense of accomplishment was not necessarily in getting all A's. If you usually got C's and got a B instead you felt like you were doing well. Nobody wanted to get an F. That meant that you had failed. Too many F's and you would have to take the class again. How much worse could it get–to retake a class you hated and failed the first time? We like to achieve and be rewarded for our achievements. This is works based living.

If your school was anything like mine, the students compared themselves with others on how well they did on the most recent test. It was usually the A students who were the most eager to show their test score. As you go down the grades the students were less and less willing to discuss how they did, let alone show anyone their paper. Unfortunately, we do not outgrow this when we finish school. We continue to compare ourselves to others; usually those that we feel are doing worse than we are. Some of us don't even outgrow it when we become Christians. Our comparisons are now based on how well we are doing spiritually. This is often based on the law and how well the other person is keeping the Christian law as we see it (Luke 18:9-14 The Pharisee and the tax collector).

God in His great mercy does not grade us who are in Christ based on our moral, righteous, and good achievements. If He really did this, we would all get F's. No amount of effort on our part could bring our F up to a passing grade. The very best of us might be able to get a zero. The vast majority would be in the negative numbers. God know us and loves us. He sent His Son to take the test for us. Jesus got 100% on the test. He lived a perfect life without sin. He also died for all our moral F's. When we come to God in faith, He puts our name on the test and credits the A to our account. Because of this we have no grounds for comparing our F with someone else's F. None of us pass on our own merit. We are all sinners before a holy God. In His mercy He showed us grace. By His mercy we can show others grace as well.

Prayer: Father is Heaven, thank You for not giving me what I deserve. Teach my heart to live in Your grace rather than trying to live on my own strength. Let me then show this same grace to those around me. The righteous will live by faith. I know that when I compare myself with others I am not only putting myself under the law, but encouraging them to do so also. Let me live by faith in the finished work of Christ and encourage others to do so also.

ON A LEASH
Observe the commands of the LORD your God, walking in his ways and revering him. Dueteronomy 8:6

Today I was riding home along the bike path and saw an amazing assortment of dogs and owners. The first dog was on a leash and being walked by its owner. The second dog was on a leash and the owner was walking next to the dog but the leash was neatly folded and the dog was carrying it in his mouth. The third owner was carrying a leash and walking next to the dog but the leash was not attached to the dog. The first dog was not only obeying the leash law but was under the guidance and protection of its owner. The last two were not fulfilling the intent of the law, but more importantly, though they were with their owners they certainly were not under the full restraint of their owners. Both of the dogs were well behaved at the moment. If a problem did arise, the dog was on its own with an owner yelling at it but unable to directly help deal with the situation.

In our Christian life we know who the master is–God Himself. We even know our connection to the master–Jesus Christ. Our problem is that we are not always walking in connection to Jesus. We think that carrying the leash ourselves will be sufficient. We have believed in Jesus sacrifice for us by faith and now we are trying to live a Christian life on our own. Galatians 3:3 "Are you so foolish? After beginning with the Spirit, are you now trying to attain your goal by human effort?" We can't rely on Jesus to lead us and guide us through the ups and downs of daily life because we don't want to be connected. Our own strength is not sufficient for living a life that is pleasing to God. Being a well-behaved, hard working, "leash carrying" Christian is not the way to follow Jesus.

Others of us act more like the dog that was walking beside the leash-carrying master but are not connected to the leash. They have believed and feel that is enough. They have secured eternity and now can go on to live the way they want to. Yes, they are often well-behaved people at least on the surface. The only times that they call on the master is when problems arise and then they call out to be rescued. This person needs to beware. I John 2:4-6 has strong words for this kind of Christian. "The man who says, 'I know him,' but does not do what he commands is a liar, and the truth is not in him. But if any one obeys his word, God's love is truly made complete in him. This is how we know we are in him: whoever claims to live in him must walk as Jesus did."

God wants us to be connected to Him all of the time not so that He can lord it over us but so that He can lead us along the path we should follow. He knows what is ahead. Often times He leads us away from the danger but there are times when He takes us through the dangers. We can always trust Him even in the midst of hard times if we stay connected to the Master. He will never leave us nor forsake us but He will take us where we need to go.

Prayer: Father, keep my heart attached to You by faith in Jesus. Don't ever let me think that I can be a Christian apart from You. Because my heart wanders easily, I ask that You always remind me of Your grace so that my heart will desire to stay connected to You. Thank You for sending Your Holy Spirit to be with me and guide me. Let me always rely on Him.

LANGUAGE LEARNING
So then, just as you received Christ Jesus as Lord, continue to live in him, rooted and built up in him, strengthened in the faith as you were taught, and overflowing with thankfulness. Colossians 2:6

When we first came to Japan we went to two years of language school. We went to school 4 hours a day, five days a week, and had 4-5 hours of homework each day. I had never studied so hard in my life. There were times when I was sure that I would never speak this seemingly impossible language. This was not what stood out to me in the long run. What really struck me was that language learning was never ending. We would finish one quarter of Japanese language study and continue the next quarter with Japanese language study. When I was in college, I took a variety of classes each quarter and the following quarter took different classes. In language study I always took Japanese. I would finish one textbook and then start the next. After two years I graduated but the studying did not stop there. I had so much more to learn that continual study was necessary. I came to realize that language learning is a continual ongoing part of living in a foreign country.

As a Christian I need to be a continual learner. There have been and will continue to be times when learning what God wants to teach is not pleasant. It is always necessary and always for my good. I will not finish the course of becoming like Christ until the day that I see Him face to face in Heaven. This doesn't need to be a discouragement to me. I can face each day with a renewed spirit knowing that the Holy Spirit is always with me to teach me and change me. I have the opportunity to experience both my need and God's love and sufficiency. Each day is an adventure with God.

When I first became a Christian I thought a lot about Psalm 137:3-4 "For there our captors asked us for songs, our tormentors demanded songs of joy; they said, 'Sing us one of the songs of Zion!' How can we sing the songs of the Lord while in a foreign land?" The Israelites were captives in a foreign land. This earth, when compared to heaven, is a foreign land for those who are in Christ. The ways that seem natural to man are like a foreign language when compared to God's ways. We are to be perpetual learners with the Holy Spirit as our teacher. Our lessons did not end when we accepted Christ as our Savior. There is only one course and that is to become like Jesus. Just as I will always have more Japanese that I need to learn, I will always need to be taught by the Holy Spirit so that the lessons sink deep into my heart and my heart begins to speak the language of heaven.

Prayer: Lord, never let me be content to stop learning from You. Make my heart into that of a continual learner. Give me a sense of adventure as I learn the new language of Christ's love. Although my pride often wants to believe that I have graduated from the school of the Holy Spirit, keep me enrolled and studying.

CITY SNOW

Cleanse me with hyssop, and I will be clean;
Wash me, and I will be whiter than snow. Psalm 51:7

Though your sins are like scarlet, they shall be as white as snow; Though they are red as crimson, they shall be like wool. Isaiah 1:18

Have you ever lived in a city? I lived in Chicago and now live in Tokyo. Chicago gets lots of snow while Tokyo only gets occasional snow but they both get city snow. It falls white and beautiful just like any other snow but it doesn't stay that way. Very quickly it gets dirty. It is not just yellow snow that is dirty. As the pollution and the car exhaust settle, the snow takes on a brownish, blackish color. You would no longer be tempted to eat it. It is not just one small area that gets dirty but all of it that gets dirty. You don't notice it happening but you do recognize that it has happened.

Our lives are very much like dirty snow. We generally do not have large dirty areas of blatant outright sins (although we may). The problem is that we do have an overall condition of sin. Our lives are not pristine and white, they are polluted by sins. These are often sins that we don't even see in ourselves. They may be things like trying to live a Christian life in our own effort, trying to earn God's love and acceptance by good works, seeking the approval of others rather than God, or living like a Christian orphan rather than a son or daughter. All of our "good efforts" are as dirty snow compared to God's holiness. In Christ, God has declared us to be holy. He wants us to rest in this truth and look to the Holy Spirit to make us like the fresh clean snow.

Perhaps the saddest part of the "dirty snow" in our lives is that we often prefer it to clean snow. If we go out and play in the snow and build a snowman we want the cleanest snow we can find. We don't want our snowman to be polluted with dirt and grass. In our own lives we are not so discriminating. We don't even see the dirty snow in our lives. If someone points it out to us, we will often become angry or defensive. God offers us white snow and we turn Him down. We would rather stay as we are than face our sins and admit to them. We are too proud to admit that all of our good works are not good enough. We don't want to humble ourselves. Letting go of our good works feels like death. What will be left of us if we let go? The amazing answer is that God will replace the dirty snow of our works with the white snow of His Holy Spirit's work. What an incredible gift from God! We are covered by Christ's righteousness.

Prayer: Lord, help me to see dirty snow in my life for what it is–sin. Show me the true blackness of sin. Teach me to know that it is not just the BIG SINS that are black but that those sins that I see as small and acceptable are just as black. Keep me ever turning to you to be cleansed and renewed. Show me the great joys of being clean in Christ rather than dirty in myself.

CREATION SINGS
We know that the whole creation has been groaning as in the pains of childbirth right up to the present time. Romans 8:22

We often take our vacation on a lake near Mt. Fuji. The lake is noted for being a good location for windsailing. On a day with good wind the lake is dotted with colorful sails bobbing in the breeze. Even on a calm day the lake is alive with ripples. On sunny days these seem to become millions of dancing points of light each praising God for His great creation.

What we see of creation is a dim reminder of what God originally created. With man's fall, creation also fell. If a lake with its dancing sunlight can be an overwhelming reminder to us of what praises to God can look like, how much more awe inspiring must the original creation have been.

Tarnished silver is black with no trace of the beauty that lies hidden. When it is polished the beauty returns to glisten in the sunlight. In the same way, our world has virtually no trace of the total beauty that was created, but God will one day remove all sin from this world and create a new world. Then the Son will shine and all of creation will praise His name.

Man also was created to praise God and fellowship with Him. We are the crowning of all of creation and we are the downfall of all of creation. When Christ came to earth and died for each one of us, He did so much more than just provide a means of forgiveness of sins. He created a means for us to have new hearts with which to praise God.

The whole of creation is groaning with a desire to praise God as He should be praised. We can praise Him but so often we don't. Does your heart sing and dance to His praise? If not, take a moment to think of some of the wonderful things for which God deserves to be praised. I'll give you a few to get you started.

His holiness	His mercy
His creative ability	His love
His majesty	His patience

Now think of a few of the hundreds of thousands of things that God has done in your life.

Given you faith to believe
Lives in you
Made you his special child for all eternity
Given you Christ's righteousness
Forgiven your sins
Given you a new heart to love Him, others, and yourself

Prayer: Father, teach my heart to sing and dance with the praise that You and You alone deserve. Don't let me ever be content with a meager PTL but let me PRAISE THE LORD with a heart that sings! Let tears come to my eyes when I contemplate Your glory. Never let me be outdone by creation's praises to You.

How to Run the Race

I have fought the good fight, I have finished the race, I have kept the faith. 2 Timothy 4:7

When I was in high school I ran low hurdles and quarter mile on the track team. I wasn't the best of runners but I was part of the team. The hardest race I ran was the 440 low hurdles. It was long enough to be grueling and the hurdles made it more so, at least in my opinion. By the end of the race it was hard to get my lead foot over the hurdle. Although it was hard, I did know how long the race was. I knew that the race was 440 yards, not 100 meters or a marathon (422,000 meters). If I ran it like I was running a marathon, I would be sure to come in last. If people ran a marathon like they were running a 100 yard dash, those watching would laugh knowing that they would never finish the race. They would use up all of their energy long before the end of the race.

Picture a race where you are not told how long it would be. It could end any moment or go on for another hour or more. You have no idea where the finish line is. How would you train for such a race? What would your strategy be while running such a race?

This is how Christians often view their Christian life. They don't understand where the goal line is or how long the race will be. Some seem to be running a steeple chase with obstacles, some run up hills and around twisting turns while others seem to run on flat smooth track. In our comparisons we get confused and discouraged. There is a sense in which it is true that we don't know how long the race will be or what it will include. We have no idea if the Lord will return tomorrow or years and years from now. We have no idea if our life will continue into old age or suddenly end. We don't know if our life will be smooth or if God will lead us through hard circumstances. How do we plan and prepare for this kind of life?

God has told us where the finish line is–to be with the Lord in heaven. He has not only told us where the finish line is but also how to run the race. We are to live a life of repentance and faith. We do not know what the future holds and how to plan for the race that is before us but the good news is that God does know the future. He knows how long the race is and what the race involves. Galatians 3:3 "Are you so foolish? After beginning with the Spirit, are you now trying to attain your goal by human effort?" By our efforts it is impossible for us to run the race that God has before us. If we live by faith, we can not only finish the race, but also run it to the glory of God. We have a choice. We can try to run the race by our own efforts and live in false confidence or fear, or we can decide daily to run the race in faith in the Son of God and live in peace and joy. I choose to run in faith. What about you?

Prayer: Father, help me to learn in ever deepening ways what it means to live in faith. Teach me to be focused on You and not on the circumstances that surround me. When I experience success, let me give credit to Your grace and when I fail, let me remember the cross of Christ Jesus. Let me always remember that by my own efforts I cannot live a righteous life, but that by faith in Christ, my Savior, I already have His righteousness. Let this truth be so strongly embedded in my heart that any thought of self-effort will quickly be replaced by a confident look to You.

THE *TSUNAMIS* OF LIFE

I have told you these things, so that in me you may have peace. In this world you will have trouble. But take heart! I have overcome the world.
John 16:33

Most of our life is like living in the quiet and calm of a beach in summer. The waves that come rolling in sometimes sweep us off our feet but generally they do more to make life interesting than to make life difficult. As with waves on the ocean there is an occasional larger wave that strikes us. Some of us live in sheltered bays where large waves are rare and some live where the big waves come crashing in. When the big wave comes we gasp for breath and ask, "Why?!!" The wave is just a wave and cannot answer. Looking back, sometimes we come to understand and sometimes we don't. Either way, we can learn to trust God who does understand. He is our lifeguard who keeps us from drowning in the circumstances of life.

Once in a rare while a *tsunami* (tidal wave) comes along and brings destruction and terror. How can we survive such power? The only place that is safe is high ground. The greater the tsunami, the higher the ground must be. The 9/11 terrorist attack in America was such a tsunami. It swept into our lives with no warning and brought its own form of destruction and fear. Where is the high ground for those of us who inherit what is left behind? The high ground is the same place that it has always been. Christ is our Savior, our hope for today, tomorrow, and for eternity. Just as a lifeguard breathes life into those he rescues, we need to run to Jesus and let Him breathe His life into us.

Jesus knows what it is to be swept away by the *tsunamis* of life. He lived a perfect, obedient life marked by love for man and for God. Yet His life was cut short by injustice, betrayal and a horrific death on the cross. He knew how it felt to be all alone when He was cut off from the Father because our sins were put on Him. Through all of this He continued to love mankind. He knew His life and death had a purpose. Without His death there could be no resurrection, no forgiveness of sins, and no redemption for mankind.

Our lives are far from being perfect. We cannot be the saviors of the world. In fact, we need Jesus to be our lifeguard every day. He tells us what is safe and rescues us when we follow our own guidance. Despite our failings, we can be God's representatives today. Because Love (Jesus) lives in us, we can go through the tsunami still loving man and God–in His power.

You have heard that it was said, "Love your neighbor and hate your enemy." But I tell you: "Love your enemies and pray for those who persecute you, that you may be sons of your Father in heaven." Matthew 5:43-45a

Prayer: Father, take this heart of mine that is so overwhelmed and breathe Your life into it. Fill my heart that is unlovable and unkind with Your amazing love not just for the lovable and kind, but also for the unlovable and the unkind. Give me a heart that can love my friends and my enemies. I honestly don't want to love my enemies, so I ask that You give me the desire to love as well as the ability to love.

MEMORY LOSS

Remember this, fix it in mind, take it to heart, you rebels. Remember the former things, those of long ago; I am God, and there is no other; I am God, and there is none like me. Isaiah 46:8-9

Toward the end of her life my mother developed cancer. Because the initial prognosis was 2-6 months, my sister and I went to stay with her. (By the way she lived for nearly 2 years.) I don't know if it was the cancer, the chemotherapy, or just old age, but she lost much of her short-term memory. Several times a day she would ask if this was Friday. We would simply say no, it was Monday or whatever day it was. Fortunately she was not upset about this. We knew she couldn't help it so we were not upset by it either. Her long-term memory was still very good. She always remembered her family.

I often seem to have short-term memory loss in my Christian life. God teaches me something that I think I will never forget. Within a surprisingly short period of time I have forgotten. What causes my memory loss? Is it unbelief, self-centeredness, pride, or one of the other idols that so often lives in my heart?

This is true not only of lesser things (short-term memory) but of essentials (long-term memory) as well. It amazes me how often I need to be reminded of my position in Christ and of how much God loves me. In one word I need to be reminded of the GOSPEL. I need to hear the Gospel from others and preach it to myself. I don't need to be embarrassed that I forget and in pride try to hide by pretending I haven't forgotten. God already knows how quickly I forget. Though my forgetting grieves Him, He still lovingly reminds me as often as I need it–daily, hourly, minute by minute.

Prayer: Father, I thank You that You remind me of my need for You. I pray that You will send Your Holy Spirit to work in my mind and in my heart to remember You, what You have done, and to trust You for what is ahead. Show me the things in my life that distract me from You, and produce in me the desire to give them to You. Help me to remember not only the things You have done long ago but to remember and live in the things that You are teaching me this day.

IDOLATRY
You shall have no other gods before me. Exodus 20:3

Idolatry is worshipping anything you use or using anything you worship. —Augustine

The most common view of idolatry is the worship of idols made of stone or wood. This was very common during Biblical times. Today it is less common but still practiced by some religions and people. In Japan it is not uncommon to see stone idols at temples and even along the street. Christians would all agree that the worship of idols (statues) is idolatry.

Over the last few years I have come to understand that idolatry also includes all of those things that we look to in order to fill the spot in our heart that only God can fill. This can be such things as money, possessions, sex, or success. It also can be such things as seeking the approval of others, pride, being a perfectionist, or being self-righteous. As Christians we might have a harder time agreeing on these as idols. We perhaps might say that yes they could be idols but we more likely would call them flaws in character or small sins. We don't want to see them in ourselves, and we definitely don't want to call them idols. Perhaps one of the most controversial idols for many of us is the idol of self-effort. Many Christians think that the phrase, "God helps them who help themselves" is from the Bible. It isn't! When we live our Christian lives as a means of earning God's blessings or of showing Him how good we are, we take God's place and worship our own efforts and accomplishments.

Look again at this quote from Augustine and think in even broader terms concerning idolatry. Is it possible to worship the one true living God and still be an idolater? Yes, I think it is. God looks at our motives, not just our actions or our words. He desires our worship but He desires it from a heart that loves Him. In my own life I'm saddened to realize that there are times when my worship is really a means of getting what I want from God. I use my good works as a means of self-gratification. This is not true worship. It is idolatry because I'm worshipping the blessings of God rather than the God of blessings, and it gives no glory to God.

When I look at my relationships with other people, I realize that what hurts the most is when I feel used by others for their own benefit. They don't care about the relationship or me. They only desire to have their own wants met. I have done this to others but what is even sadder is that I do this to God when I worship Him only as a means of gaining my desires. If I worship God as a means of using Him to meet my needs; it is not only sad; it is idolatry.

Prayer: Lord, keep me from idolatry even when the idolatry looks good on the outside. Give me a heart that can distinguish true worship from idolatry. Let me always praise You for who You are and not just what You do. Fill my heart to over-flowing with Your amazing grace. Let the light of Your Gospel so shine in my heart that I will always desire You rather than idols.

The Top of the Mountain

This is what the Lord says: "Stand at the crossroads and look; ask for the ancient paths, ask where the good way is and walk in it, and you will find rest for your souls. But you said, 'We will not walk in it.'" Jeremiah 6:16

"And now, O Israel, what does the Lord your God ask of you but to fear the Lord your God, to walk in all his ways, to love him, to serve the Lord your God with all your heart and with all your soul," Deuteronomy 10:12

When John and I were first married we would go for walks together. I remember on our honeymoon we walked part way up the grassy slopes of a mountain in Jackson Hole, Wyoming. My goal was to get exercise by power walking. John's goal was to enjoy my company and look at the flowers and plants as we strolled along. If I am hiking on a mountain I want to get to the top of the mountain. I am not terribly interested in the scenery as I go but I do look forward to the view from the top. John is not so much interested in reaching the top, as he is interested in the process. Needless to say this was not the best combination. We finally gave up taking walks together unless we set the ground rules. Before we left we would decide if we were walking for exercise or for enjoyment. It seemed like a reasonable solution but looking back at it I am saddened to realize how wrong I was and how much I missed. Yes, there are times for exercise but how much more there need to be times of companionship and strolling.

My Christian life has been much the same. I set my goals and off I go toward what I see as the top of my mountain. Because I am so focused on reaching the goal, I often forget to take my hiking partner with me. I leave God somewhere behind me as I press on to the goal. God is more interested in the process of my life and seemingly less interested in the task at hand. My problem is that I don't realize that the task at hand is the process of living life with the Father. My getting to the top of the mountain will not please Him if I have left Him behind. Unlike John, God will not compromise spending time with me. He will not allow me to set the ground rules. He already has set them and He wants me to learn to follow them. The ground rules are to show me His love and caring concern so my heart will learn to trust and love Him. Spending time with God who loves me as I follow the path He has set for me is so much better than going through life alone–no matter how successful I may feel when I reach my goal. Sometimes the path along which God leads me is not the most direct route to the top, but it will always be the best route.

Prayer: Father, I know You are always with me to be my walking companion, but in my pride, independence, and self-centeredness I forget and go on without You. Remind me that it is You who is important and not what I get done. Keep my focus on You and the process that You are taking me through. Teach me to desire You and enjoy Your company through each moment of my life now and forever.

WHICH WILL IT BE?

My people have committed two sins: They have forsaken me, the spring of living water, and have dug their own cisterns, broken cisterns that cannot hold water. Jeremiah 2:13

We moved to Higashi Kurume City, Japan more than 15 years ago. At that time there was a small river that we often walked along on our way to language school. We could see sudsy laundry water flowing into the river. There would be areas where the stench of the water was almost overwhelming. There was very little wildlife in the water, as it was becoming more and more polluted. No one was allowed to swim or wade in the river; no one would want to either. I can't imagine anyone wanting to drink water out of this very polluted river.

Just an hour or two away by train you can hike in the mountains. In these mountains you will find streams that are clean and pure and provide cold refreshing water that anyone would want to drink. The only problem is that you have to work to get to them. These streams are not for the lazy, the easily discouraged or the casual. You have to make a determined effort to reach them. When you do, you will find that it was worth the effort and that now you really are thirsty.

Our spiritual life is very much like these two rivers. There is the easy way that seems right to many and doesn't take a lot of effort. It is convenient and seems comfortable. The problem with the easy way is that it is polluted. It doesn't refresh us but rather leads to additional struggles. A person who sees a polluted stream does not want to drink from it. If a person does and survives, then he begins to think that everything is OK. It gets easier and easier to accept the polluted as safe, the tainted as clean.

The second stream represents a life in Christ. It is refreshing and pure. It brings with it abundant life but it is not always easy. It may require hard choices and sacrifices. This life in Christ will require us to change. Most, if not all of us do not like change, especially if that change is in our hearts. We would much rather blame the other person, or our circumstances, or fate, or ignore everything rather than admit to ourselves and to God that we are in need of a heart cleansing. We don't have to be great climbers or hikers to reach the fresh streams of Christ. We do have to be willing to give up drinking the polluted water that comes from our own thinking and drink of the new water that Jesus offers. Our need for this new water is not limited to the time when we accepted Christ as our Savior. We need this new water every day of our lives.

Which stream do you want to drink from–the one that brings the greatest joy and peace or some other? The mountain stream is pure and refreshing but not easily reached. The stream running near our house is dirty but convenient. Do we want God's sanctification through faith and diligence or do we want to stay where we are and be at ease? I so often want both–God and ease. This is the struggle of my heart growth.

Prayer: Yes, Lord, give me Christ. Let me be so enraptured by the love Christ showed when He gave up all in order to win me that I will choose Christ even when it goes against what I see as my best interests. Help me to pick up my cross and follow You. Don't let my heart be content with the things that so easily satisfy. Capture my heart so I will climb the mountains and search for the pure refreshment that can only come from You.

ETERNITY WITH A STRANGER

But when the time had fully come, God sent his Son, born of a woman, born under law, to redeem those under law, that we might receive the full rights of sons. Because you are sons, God sent the Spirit who calls out, "Abba, Father." So you are no longer a slave, but a son; and since you are a son, God has made you also an heir. Galatians 4:4-7

I have a brother who is eleven years older than I am. By the time I have childhood memories he was in college. For years my view of our relationship was that of uncle and niece. He came to visit us and we went to visit him, but there was a distance rather than the closeness of shared memories that I had with my other brother and sister. Many Christians have this same kind of relationship with God. They know in their heads that God is their Father but they relate to Him like their heavenly uncle. It's nice to see Him occasionally and keep in touch but everything is very much on the surface.

God is our heavenly Father, not a long lost uncle or second cousin twice removed. He loves us not just from the distance of Heaven but lives in us through the Holy Spirit. He knows us better than we know ourselves. He knows those fears we have that we won't even face. He knows our joys and our pains. He chose us, despite who we are, out of His grace. He knows us and loves us completely and desires that we know Him also.

As an adult, my brother and I have become like brother and sister. I am so thankful that this relationship has become closer. The same is true of my relationship with God. I am learning more and more that God is not my heavenly uncle! He is my

Heavenly Father. I want as much of God as He is willing to give me. I don't want material things or blessings from Him. (Although these things are nice.) I want to know God and let that relationship grow and grow for the rest of my days on this Earth. I don't want to spend Eternity with a stranger. I want to spend Eternity with my best friend, brother, father. Eternity starts now as I learn to know and love God even as I am known.

Prayer: Father teach my heart the wonder of knowing You as my Heavenly Father. Give me an ever-growing desire to know You more. Let this desire be for You and not just for the things You can do for me. Help me to appreciate the things You do all around me but especially let me be thankful for the work You do in my heart. Please don't ever let me take You for granted. Let Eternity begin today in that I am with You, my Heavenly Father who loves me.

It Is Finished

When he had received the drink, Jesus said, "It is finished." With that, he bowed his head and gave up his spirit. John 19:30

I have been working on a large cross-stitch picture and I am looking forward to the day when I can say, "It is finished." Most of the time it has been enjoyable to work on, especially as I think about the joy that it will give the receiver. But there have been times when it seems like just another project that I have to get finished.

My daughter is a senior in high school. I know she is looking forward to June when she can say, "I am finished." Have you ever been to a graduation and seen the looks of joy and relief on the faces of the graduates? The unknown is ahead of them but they have finished a task that has taken years to complete. There have been times of enjoyment and times of struggle but they have endured and have finished.

Generally we do not say, "It is finished" unless it has taken us a long time to finish or it has required a lot of effort and struggle to finish. Often times it has been both. We rejoice that we have accomplished what we set out to do but also that we can go on to do something else.

When Jesus was on the cross His last words were, "It is finished." He had spent three years in trying to reach the hearts of the world as a servant. More than that, He had spent 33 years living on this earth, separated from Heaven. Even before that, He knew from the beginning of time that the cross was in His future. He knew that He would need to give His life in order for mankind to receive forgiveness, be made right with God, and be given eternal life with the Father. There was great joy and tremendous sorrow mixed together when He said it was finished. Yes there was joy in knowing that all He had gone through was going to be finished. But there was also heart-breaking pain because physically He was dying and spiritually He was being totally separated from the Father. The moment God put our sins on Jesus, for those moments, Jesus could no longer fellowship with the One He had spent eternity with. How incredibly long that separation must have felt! Praise God it is finished and we too can enjoy the finished work of Christ.

To the disciples there was no joy at all in hearing Jesus say that it was finished. Their hopes were dashed and God must have seemed to be far away. They didn't know that in just three days He would rise from the dead and they would see Him again. They didn't know that He would return to Heaven the victor and would send the Holy Spirit to dwell in each one of them so they (and each one of us) could have continual uninterrupted fellowship with God. They didn't know the joys and struggles that were ahead of them because of the finished work of Christ.

Prayer: Teach me to rejoice in Your finished work but also to rejoice in the unfinished work that You are doing in my heart. I look forward to the day that I will stand before You complete in Christ's righteousness and know that I truly am finished.

THE SEVEN MILLION DOLLAR GIFT

Thanks be to God for his indescribable gift! 2 Corinthians 9:15
the unsearchable riches of Christ. Ephesians 3:8b

The other day I watched a program on Cartier, the jeweler, and the empire he built. During the program they mentioned that they had recently made an item that, if I remember correctly, cost seven million dollars. I can't imagine something costing that much. Obviously, this customer could and did. I got to thinking about this piece of jewelry. Suppose it was a gift. What a gift! I'm sure the recipient said thank you.

I have never received a seven million dollar piece of jewelry and I never want to. I have received a number of gifts over the years. I hate to admit it but I have been rather poor at writing thank you notes. I appreciated and still appreciate the gifts. In my head I have dictated beautiful thank you letters. Unfortunately they don't always get written, so the giver may never know how thankful I am and how often I think of him/her/them.

I have received a gift that is beyond price–several in fact–my parents, brothers, sister, husband, children, and many friends. These relationships cannot be bought or sold. Their value is beyond what even the wealthiest can afford. Yet they are available to even the poorest amongst us. Too often I fail to realize how great their value is. Even when I do realize their value, I fail to let the people know how thankful I am.

There is another gift that I have received that is even more valuable. This is the gift of Jesus Christ, God's own Son. But God did not stop at this gift of eternal life. He also gave us His Holy Spirit to live in each of us who believe in the Son. God's gift is not just one wonderful gift but daily and hourly gifts. He shares Himself with us! The creator of the universe shares Himself with us His creation. He pours out His love on us and through us to others. He transforms us, the unloving and unlovable, into the image of Christ so that we can love God and love others. He gives us the righteousness of Christ. He gives us hope for real change in us, not just in our circumstances.

Do I value and appreciate these gifts, as I should? Do I live a life of thanksgiving to my heavenly Father? Just as I must confess to being a poor thank you writer, I must confess that I don't sufficiently appreciate what God has done, is doing, and will do. As a sinner it is not possible to adequately appreciate God. My prayer is that God will teach my heart to be more appreciative and thankful.

Prayer: Thank You heavenly Father for the gift of Your Son, Jesus Christ. Thank You also for sending Your Holy Spirit to live in my life. Each day You give gifts that I don't even notice but I want to thank You for them. I pray that You will work in my heart to make me more aware of the work that You are doing in and around me. I also pray that You will give me a heart that overflows with thankfulness to You the giver of all good things.

CAN YOU SEE THE STARS?

And there were shepherds living out in the fields nearby, keeping watch over their flocks at night. An angel of the Lord appeared to them, and the glory of the Lord shone around them, and they were terrified. But the angel said to them, "Do not be afraid. I bring you good news of great joy that will be for all the people. Today in the town of David a Savior has been born to you; he is Christ the Lord. This will be a sign to you: You will find a baby wrapped in cloths and lying in a manger." Luke 2:8-12

When I was a child I lived in a small town in Iowa. I remember summer evenings of looking at the stars. The sky was alight with little pins of light. I can't say that I thought deeply about them but simply enjoyed them being there.

I grew up and moved to the city. I no longer take the time to look at the night sky. I stay in my house and watch the lights from our TV instead. Even if I went out and looked, I wouldn't see very many stars because the lights from the city prevent me from seeing them. They are still there but it is not dark enough to see them.

With Christmas season I think of the shepherds who were out in their fields taking care of their sheep. The sky was full of stars. I don't know if they noticed them on that very special night, but they did see the glory of God shine around them. The angel was announcing the birth of the King of kings and the Lord of lords–the Savior of the world. They left their flocks and their work, and went to see the child born in Bethlehem. Their hearts were full of wonder and amazement.

As a child I enjoyed the stars in the sky and the story of the birth of Jesus. I didn't really think of them together though. When I first became a Christian I remember seeing the stars with fresh eyes. I not only saw stars afresh but I also saw the darkness of my own sin. Without seeing the darkness of sin I couldn't see the brightness of Christ. The stars were not only beautiful, but reminded me of my Savior who loved me enough to come to earth, live a perfect life, die on the cross, and rise again to provide a way to the Father.

As the years passed I became busier (or at least thought I was) and my spiritual life became drier. I served the Lord as a means of earning His blessings, but my eyes no longer saw the beauty of the night sky and my heart no longer felt the amazement of my Savior's love. Christmas became a favorite season but the wonder of the season was often missing. Just as only the brightest stars are visible in the city, so only the quietest moments of the season could break through my busyness.

I still live in the city and can see very few stars but my heart has returned to the place of wonder in Christ. My prayer is that I may always see the glory of the Lord born in a manger but surrounded by all the lights of the heavens.

Prayer: Father, never let me think I have outgrown my need for Christ's righteousness and so lose the wonder of Jesus' birth. May Christmas and every season bring the brightness of Christ into my heart and life and may You shine there throughout the year. May Your life shine in me and through me like a star in the darkness.

New Years in Japan

He came to that which was his own, but his own did not receive him.
John 1:11

In Japan families travel home to spend the New Year with their parents and family. New Years is similar to Thanksgiving and Christmas put together as the trains, the planes, and the roads are filled to beyond capacity. It is a quiet time of fellowship and eating New Years treats. It is almost unheard of for a family member to be turned away. (Occasionally when a person becomes a Christian the family will disown him/her to the point that they are no longer welcome at New Years.) Family is a strong glue that holds Japanese society together.

God created man to be in relationships; the strongest of these is often family. He also created man to be in relationship with Himself. In the Old Testament the Jews were God's chosen people. Jesus left His home with the Father and came to His own but they did not welcome Him. They had decided that He would come as a political king and rescue them physically from their hardships. Instead Jesus came as a servant to save them from spiritual death. God knew that what the people wanted was only a temporary solution to an eternal problem. What He gave them was an eternal solution that could change them for the present as well as for eternity.

When I became a Christian I received Jesus as my Savior and

He received me into His family. He will never turn me away and tell me that I am no longer welcome. He always wants to spend time with me. I am not as faithful as I go through times of drifting away from Him and am swallowed by the busyness of life. Jesus is always waiting for my return to Him. It doesn't have to be on special holidays or even in certain religious ways. He is always waiting with open arms to receive my repentant heart.

How very sad that even today His own do not always receive Him. As I start this new year, I want to come home to Jesus in a fresh way with a heart that once again enjoys the present with God and looks forward to the day that I will go home to spend eternity with Jesus, my Savior. John 1:12 "Yet to all who received him, to those who believed in his name, he gave the right to become children of God." We are God's children not based on our faithfulness but because God has declared us to be His children. I want to start this day and this new year with an awareness that as a child of the King I am greatly loved and through Christ I can greatly love others. I want to receive my Savior and all that He wishes to do in my life. I pray that this would be true for each one of us.

Prayer: Heavenly Father, I thank You that You did send Jesus to pay for the sins of the world (including my sins) even knowing that the Israelites would reject him. I thank You that You did not give up on mankind in general or me specifically but that in Your great love You sent Your Holy Spirit to work in the sinful heart of mankind (and me) so that we could receive Your Son. Forgive me for all of the times that I have been too busy or too distracted or too self-centered to receive all that You have for me. In faith I receive Your Son afresh and ask that the wonder of His love for me would capture my heart affections and keep them on You this year. I ask that You continue to work in my heart to make me into the child that You created me to be.

Index of Themes

Christmas
    Can You See the Stars? 108
Contentment in Christ
    A Single or A Double 24
    A Wild Goose Chase 54
    Bad Attitude 44
Easter
    It Is Finished 104
Idol Worship (Heart Idols)
    Creation or The Creator 12
    Idolatry 96
    The Garden 46
    The Tapioca Incident 28
    Tree Removal 78
Joy in Christ
    A New Day 10
    Unspeakable Joy 58
    What Is Going On? 26
Living by Faith
    How To Run The Race 90
    Sin and the Computer Virus 62
    To Water or Not to Water 42
    When Sight Is Faith 16
Living in Christ
    A Darkened Room 14
    A Lamp Unto My Feet 48
    No "A" Students 80

Loving God
    Engagements   20
    Eternity with a Stranger   102
    New Years in Japan   110
    The Smell of Smoke   66
    The Top of the Mountain   98
    Whitewater Rafting   72
Loving Others
    "Glad to See Ya"   22
    Right in Their Own Eyes   56
Praising God
    Creation Sings   88
    The Whole Earth Shall Praise His Name   36
Pride/Humility
    Sniff It Don't Drink It   18
Repentance
    City Snow   86
    Mission Impossible   70
    The Garden   46
    The Stench of Sin   52
Self-effort
    Knots   34
    On A Leash   82
Spiritual Growth
    Archaeology   50
    Elective Surgery   76
    Language Learning   84
    Memory Loss   94
    Shall We Dance?   32
    The Branch Cut Off   60
    Thoughts Along the Way   8
Spiritual Refreshment
    Can You See the Stars?   108
    Grandpa's Lap   30
    The Freshness of Spring   40
    Water for Our Souls   68
    Which Will It Be?   100
Thankfulness
    The Seven Million Dollar Gift   106
Trusting God
    On the Wings of Eagles   38
    Take Your Breath Away   74
    The Eddies of Life   64
    The Tsunamis of Life   92

INDEX OF SCRIPTURE

Genesis	50:20	Elective Surgery	76
Exodus	20:3	Idolatry	96
	29:18b	The Smell of Smoke	66
Numbers	6:24-26	Tree Removal	78
		A New Day	10
	14:18a	Bad Attitude	44
Deuteronomy	1:34-35, 39	When Sight Is Faith	16
	10:12	The Top of the Mountain	98
	11:19	Thoughts Along the Way	8
I Chronicles	16:23-25a	The Whole Earth Shall Praise His Name	36
Psalms	1:3	The Freshness of Spring	40
	5:11	Unspeakable Joy	58
	20:7-8	The Eddies of Life	64
	30:11,12	Shall We Dance?	32
	51:7	City Snow	86
	51:1-12	The Stench of Sin	52
	56:4	Whitewater Rafting	72
	62:1	Grandpa's Lap	30
	91:1	Grandpa's Lap	30
	104:1	The Whole Earth Shall Praise His Name	36
	119:105	A Lamp Unto My Feet	48
	137:3-4	Language Learning	84
	149:3-4a	Shall We Dance?	32
Proverbs	14:12	Right In Their Own Eyes	56
	17:22	What Is Going On?	26
	21:2	Right In Their Own Eyes	56
Isaiah	1:18	City Snow	86

Isaiah	30:15	Bad Attitude	44
	40:30-31	On the Wings of Eagles	38
	46:8-9	Memory Loss	94
	58:11b	To Water or Not to Water	42
Jeremiah	2:13	Which Will It Be?	100
	6:16	The Top of the Mountain	98
	17:7-8	The Freshness of Spring	40
	29:11	Knots	34
Hosea	6:6	The Smell of Smoke	66
Habakkuk	1:5	Take Your Breath Away	74
	3:2	Take Your Breath Away	74
Matthew	5:43-45a	The Tsunamis of Life	92
	7:9-11	A Single or A Double	24
	15:8-9	The Smell of Smoke	66
Mark	12:33	The Smell of Smoke	66
Luke	2:8-12	Can You See the Stars?	108
	18:9-14	No "A" Students	80
John	1:11,12	New Years in Japan	110
	3:19-21	A Lamp Unto My Feet	48
	4:13-14	Water for Our Souls	68
	14:16-18	Sin and the Computer Virus	62
	15:4-5	The Branch Cut Off	60
	16:33	The Tsunamis of Life	92
	19:30	It Is Finished	104
Romans	1:25	Creation or the Creator	12
	3:10	To Water or Not to Water	42
	3:22-24	No "A" Students	80
	8:22	Creation Sings	88
	8:22-23	The Whole Earth Shall Praise His Name	36
	8:28	Knots	34
I Corinthians	13:12	Creation or the Creator	12
II Corinthians	2:15a	The Smell of Smoke	66
	9:15	The Seven Million Dollar Gift	106
Galatians	3:3	On A Leash	82
		How to Run the Race	90
	4:4-7	Eternity with a Stranger	102
Ephesians	3:8b	The Seven Million Dollar Gift	106
Philippians	3:7-9	Sniff It Don't Drink It	18
	4:4	Mission Impossible	70
Colossians	2:6	Language Learning	84
I Thessalonians	2:16-17	A Wild Goose Chase	54
II Timothy	4:7	How to Run the Race	90
Hebrews	3:13-14	Archaeology	50
	13:1-2	"Glad to See Ya"	22
James	4:1-3	The Tapioca Incident	28
I Peter	4:9	"Glad to See Ya"	22
I John	1:5-7	A Darkened Room	14
	2:4-6	On A Leash	82
	5:21	The Garden	46
Revelation	19:7	Engagements	20
	21:4	Elective Surgery	76

Order Form

To order additional copies of this book, please use a copy of the following form.

Name _____

Address _____

City _____

State/Prov./Ken _____ Postal Code _____

Country _____

E-mail _____ Phone _____

      1-9 copies   US$5.00
      10 or more   US$4.00 each

Shipping

USA and Canada: $1.50 1st copy (each additional copy add $0.50)
Rest of World: $2.00 1st copy (each additional copy add $0.75)

Send a copy of this form with your US dollar check or money order made out to Elaine Mehn to:

    Gospel Rest Resources
    3215 E. State St.
    Rockford, IL 61108
    USA

For those living in Japan inquire at Gospel Rest Resources either by e-mail or regular mail for address and yen amount.

Order by e-mail: **GospelRestResources@Yahoo.com** or
        URL: **http://www.geocities.com/GospelRestResources**
Payment can be either in dollars or in yen. Inquire for current yen amount.